© 2024
Editor, publisher: Cornelia Kandler,
55278 Friesenheim, Germany

Photos, photomontages, illustrations,
layout, cover: Cornelia Kandler

bitundgraphit.de

All rights reserved

ISBN 979 839 926 617 6

Herausgeberin: Cornelia Kandler,
55278 Friesenheim, Deutschland

Fotos, Fotomontagen, Illustrationen, Layout,
Cover: Cornelia Kandler

bitundgraphit.de

Alle Rechte vorbehalten

Lost (and other) Places
with ballet

Lost places

'Lost places' or "lost places"
are places that were once alive and used,
but have been abandoned and left to decay
over time.
They often tell stories from the past and
are characterized by a melancholic beauty.
The fascination with 'lost places' lies in
their mysterious atmosphere.

They are combined with other fascinating
backgrounds.

Magic and mysterious beauty, what could
be more obvious than combining it with
ballet?

Let yourself be enchanted by the magic of
the images.

Verlorene Plätze

'Lost Places' oder "verlorene Plätze"
sind Orte, die einst lebendig und genutzt
waren, aber im Laufe der Zeit verlassen
und dem Verfall überlassen wurden.
Oft erzählen sie Geschichten aus der
Vergangenheit und sind von einer
melancholischen Schönheit geprägt.
Die Faszination für 'lost places' liegt in
ihrer geheimnisvollen Atmosphäre.

Kombiniert werden sie mit weiteren
faszinierenden Hintergründen.

Magie und geheimnisvolle Schönheit, was
liegt naheliegender, als es mit Ballett zu
verbinden?

Lass dich von der Magie der Bilder
verzaubern.

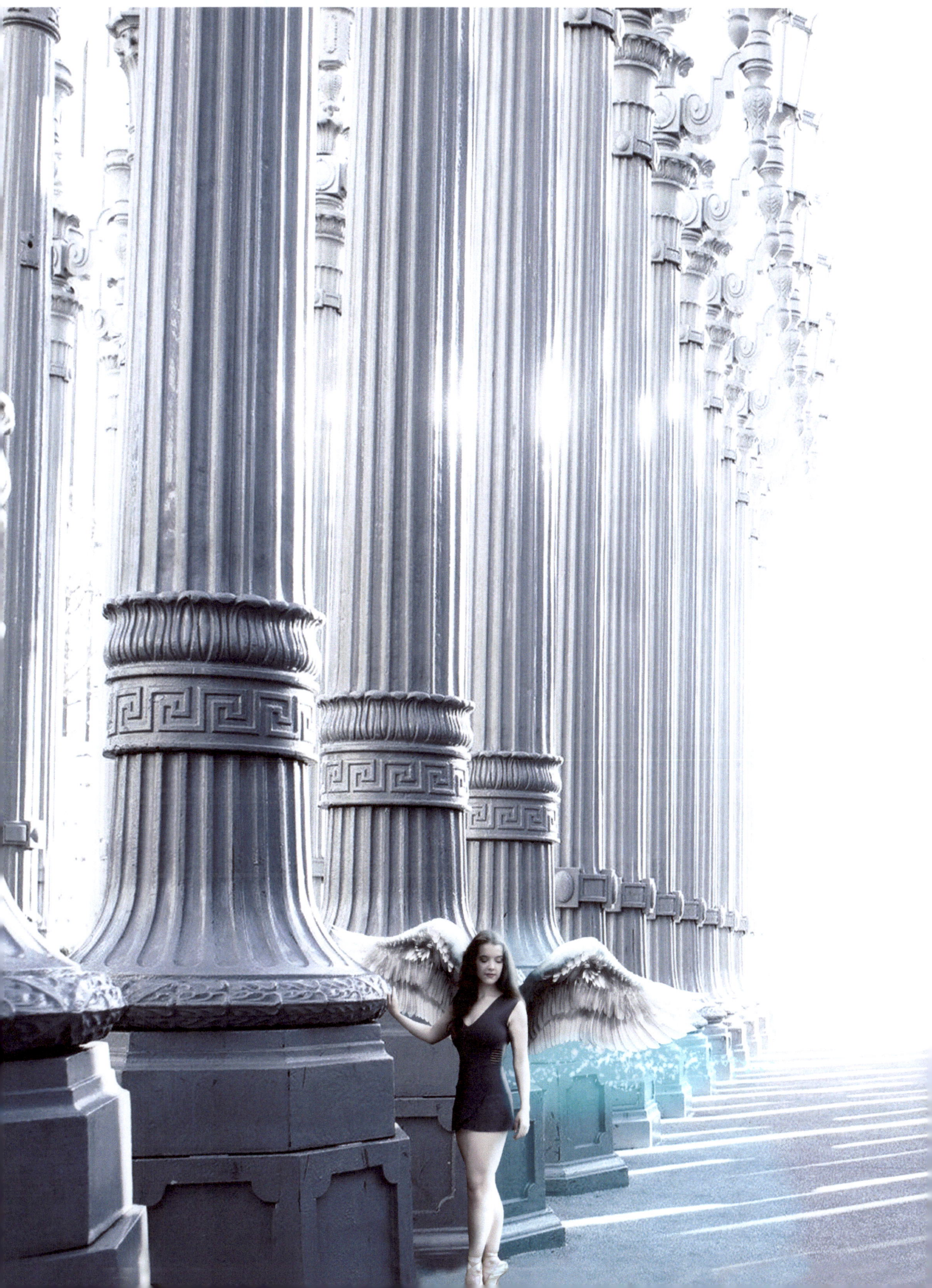

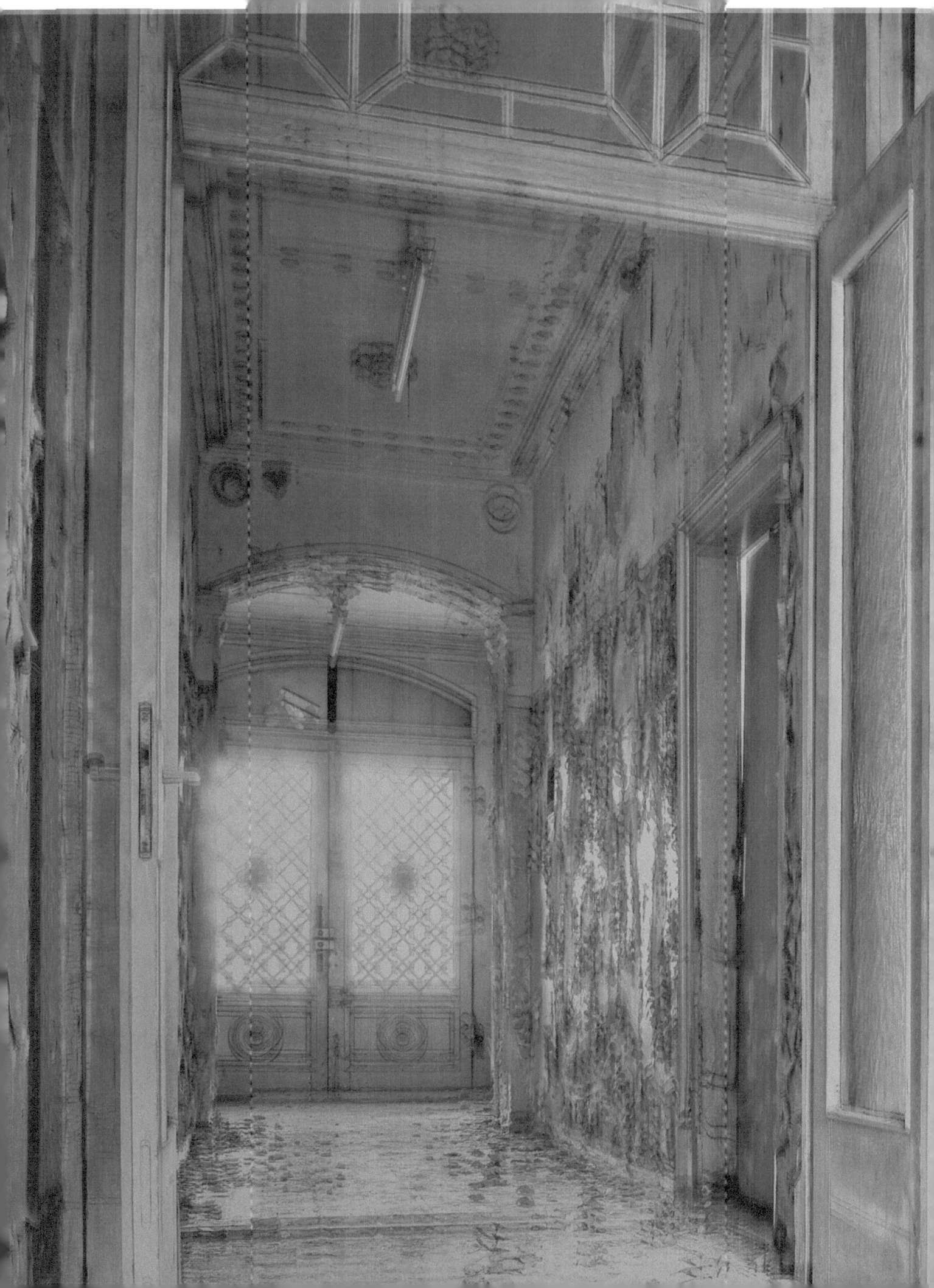

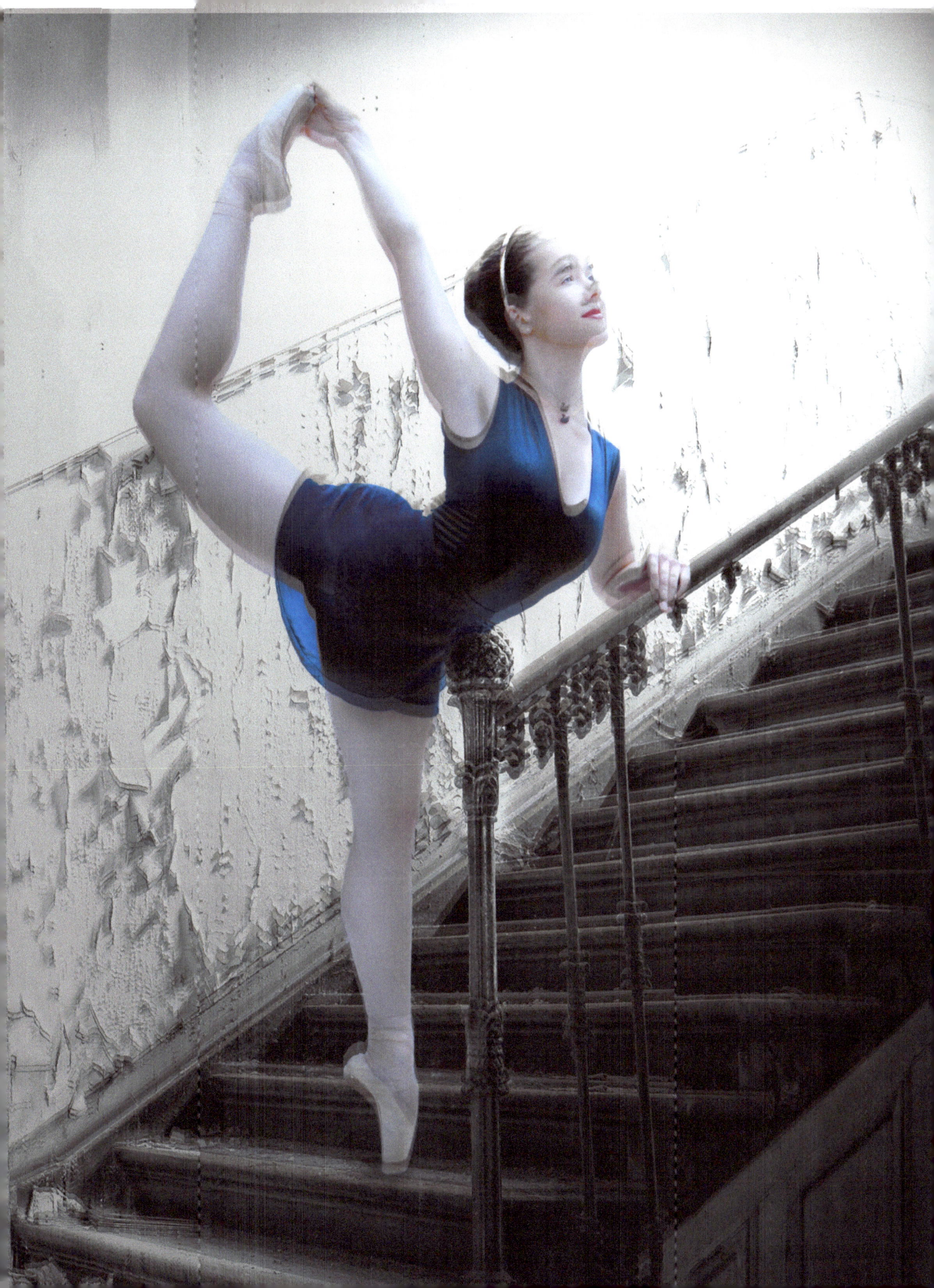

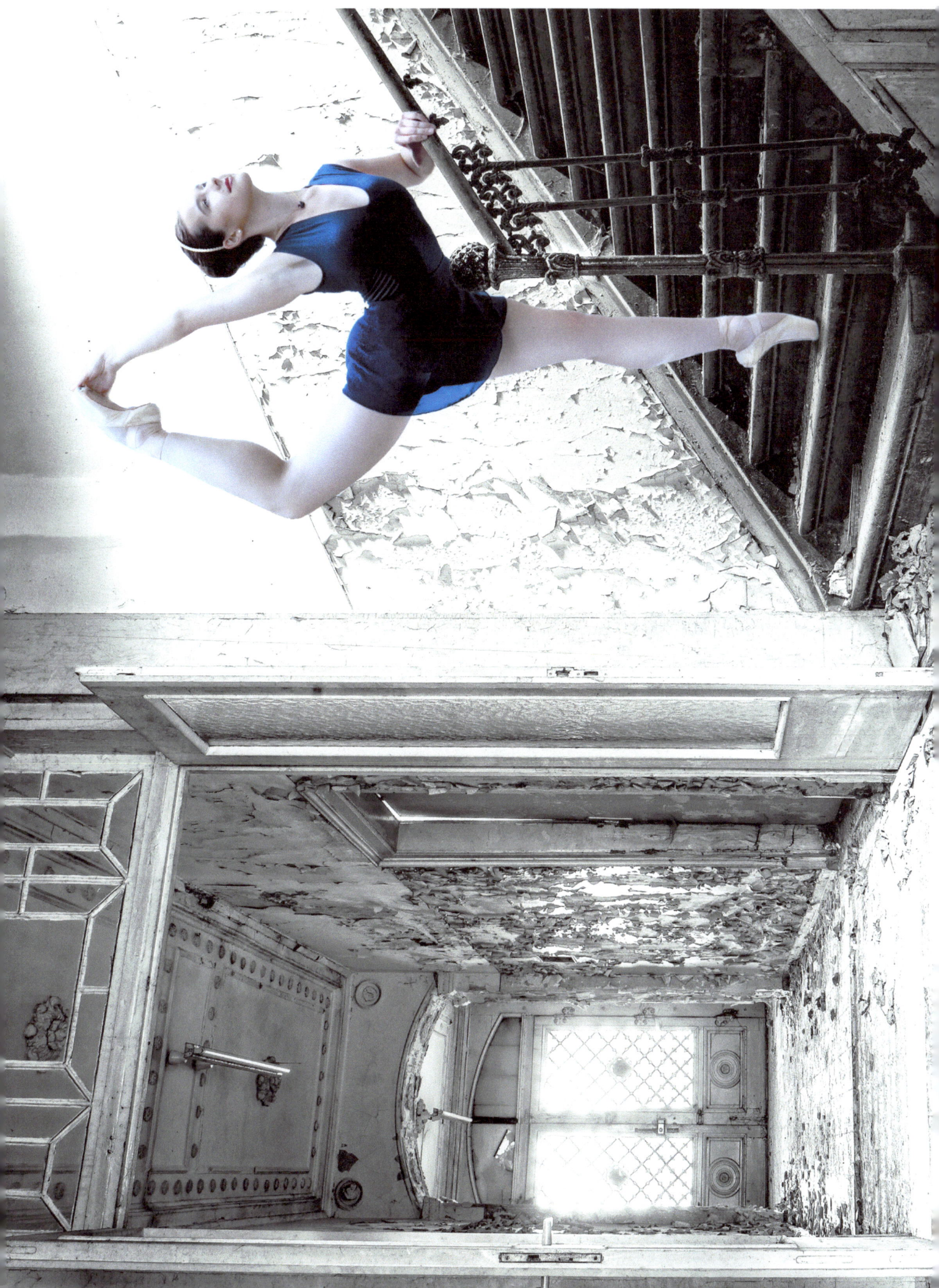

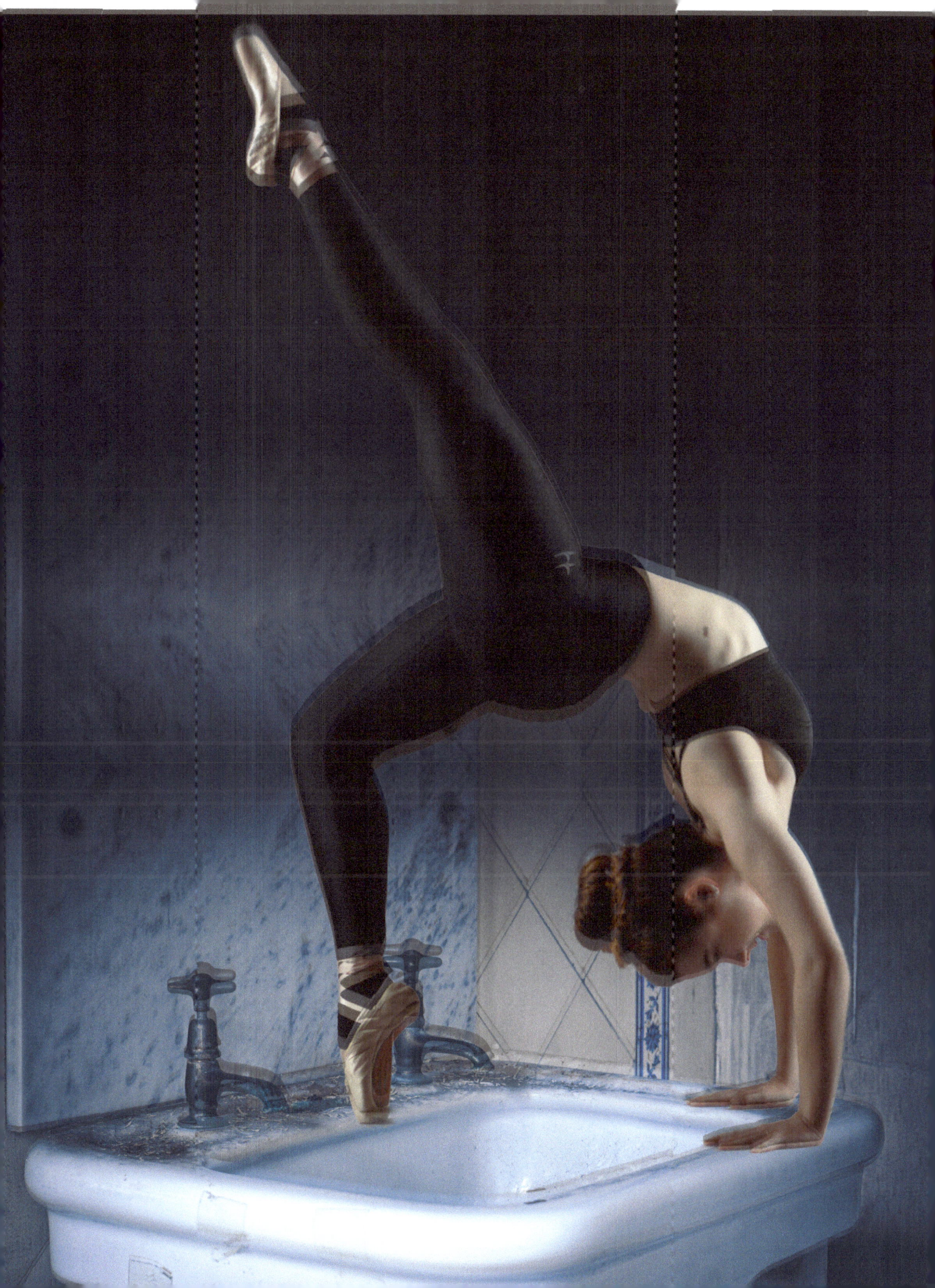

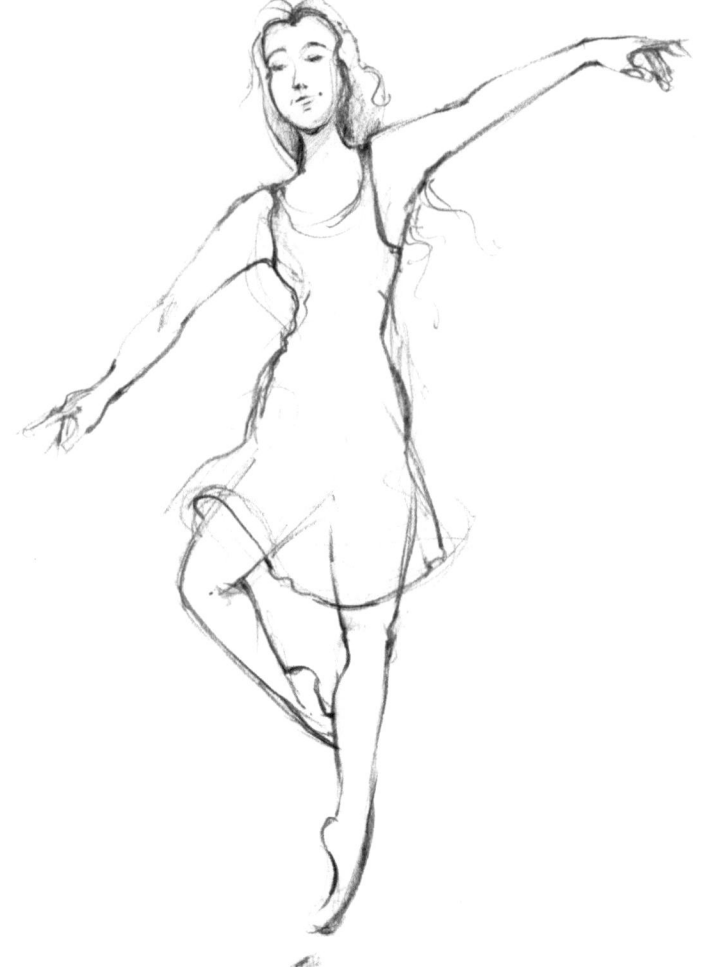

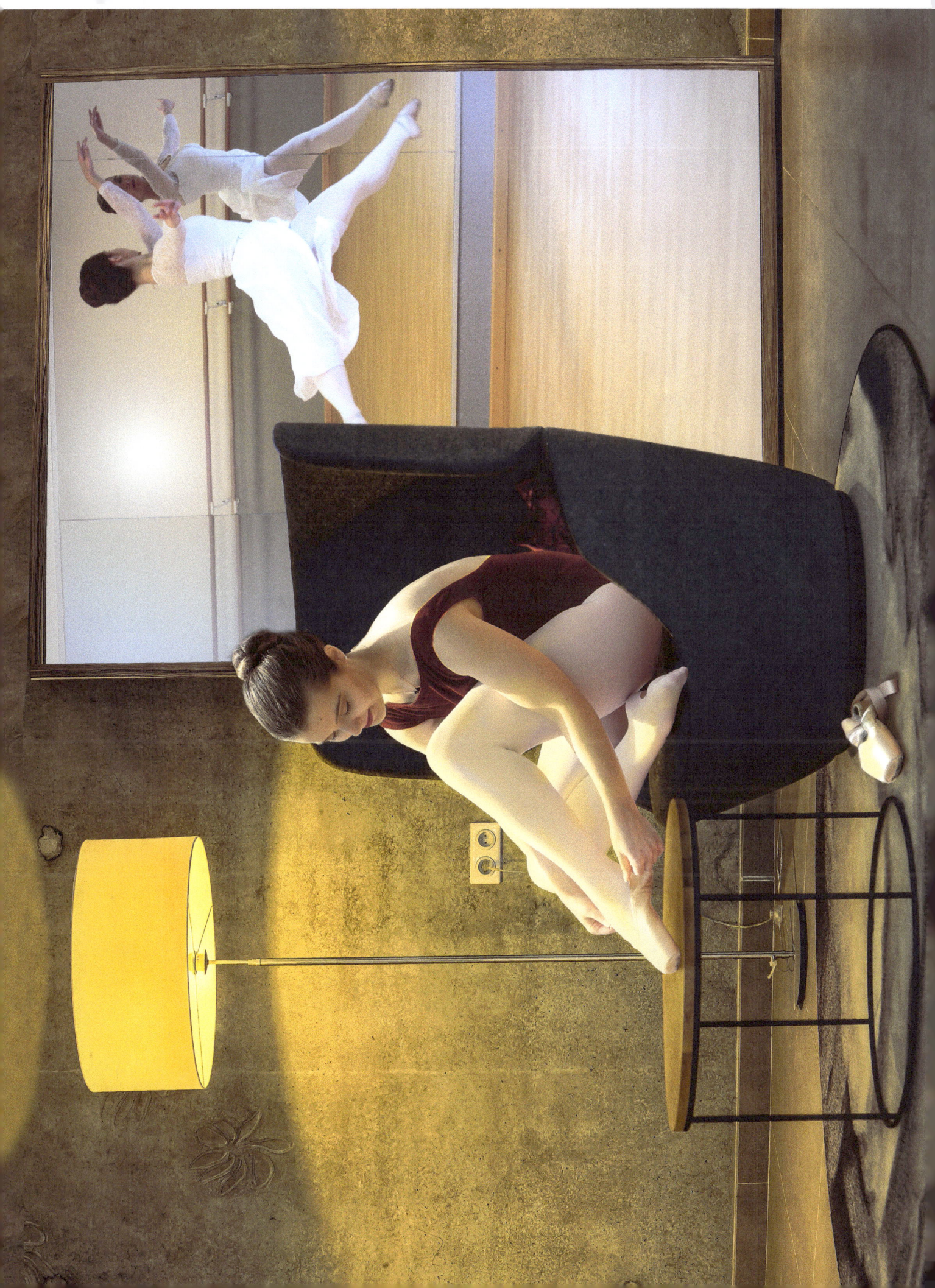

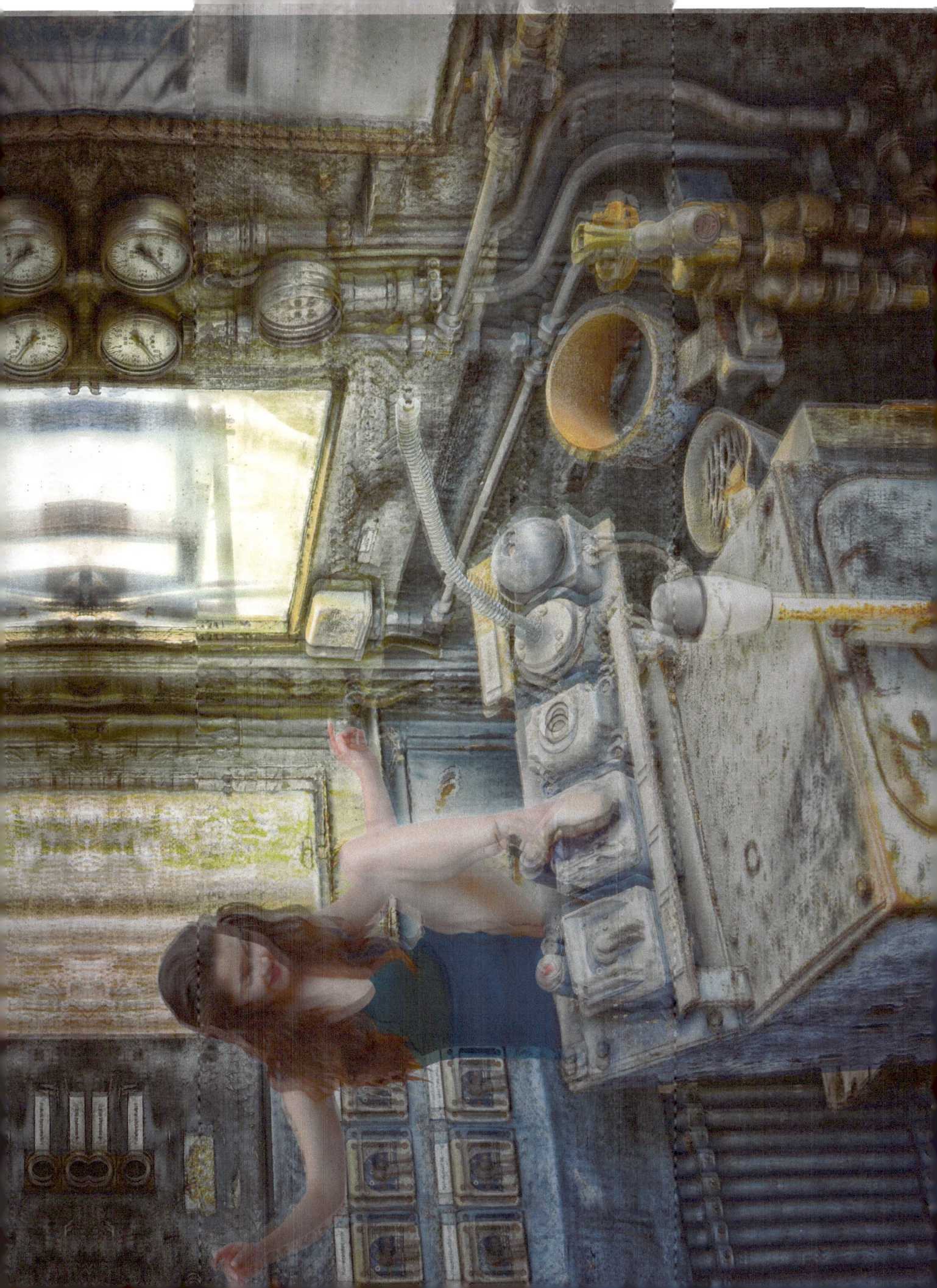

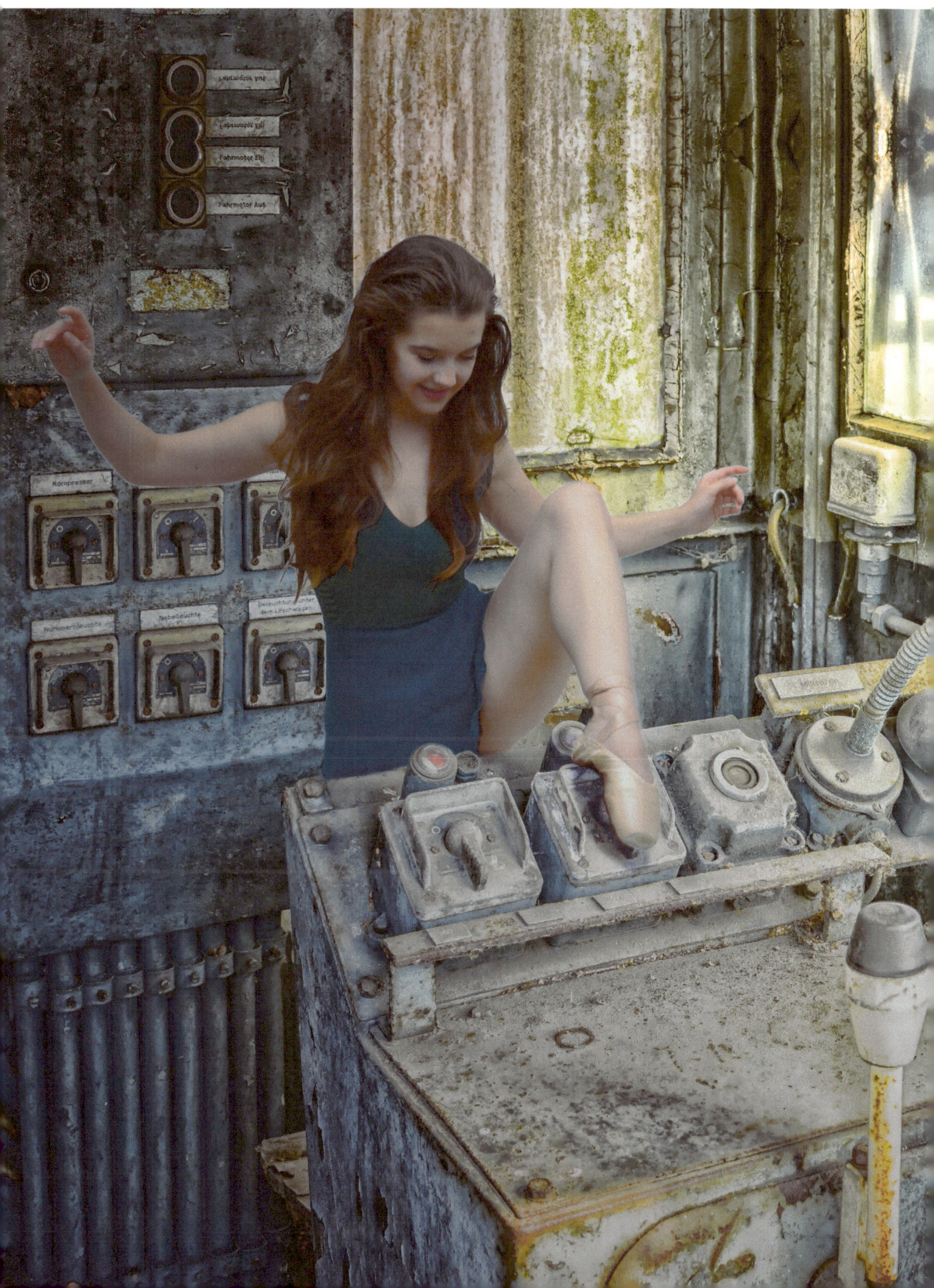

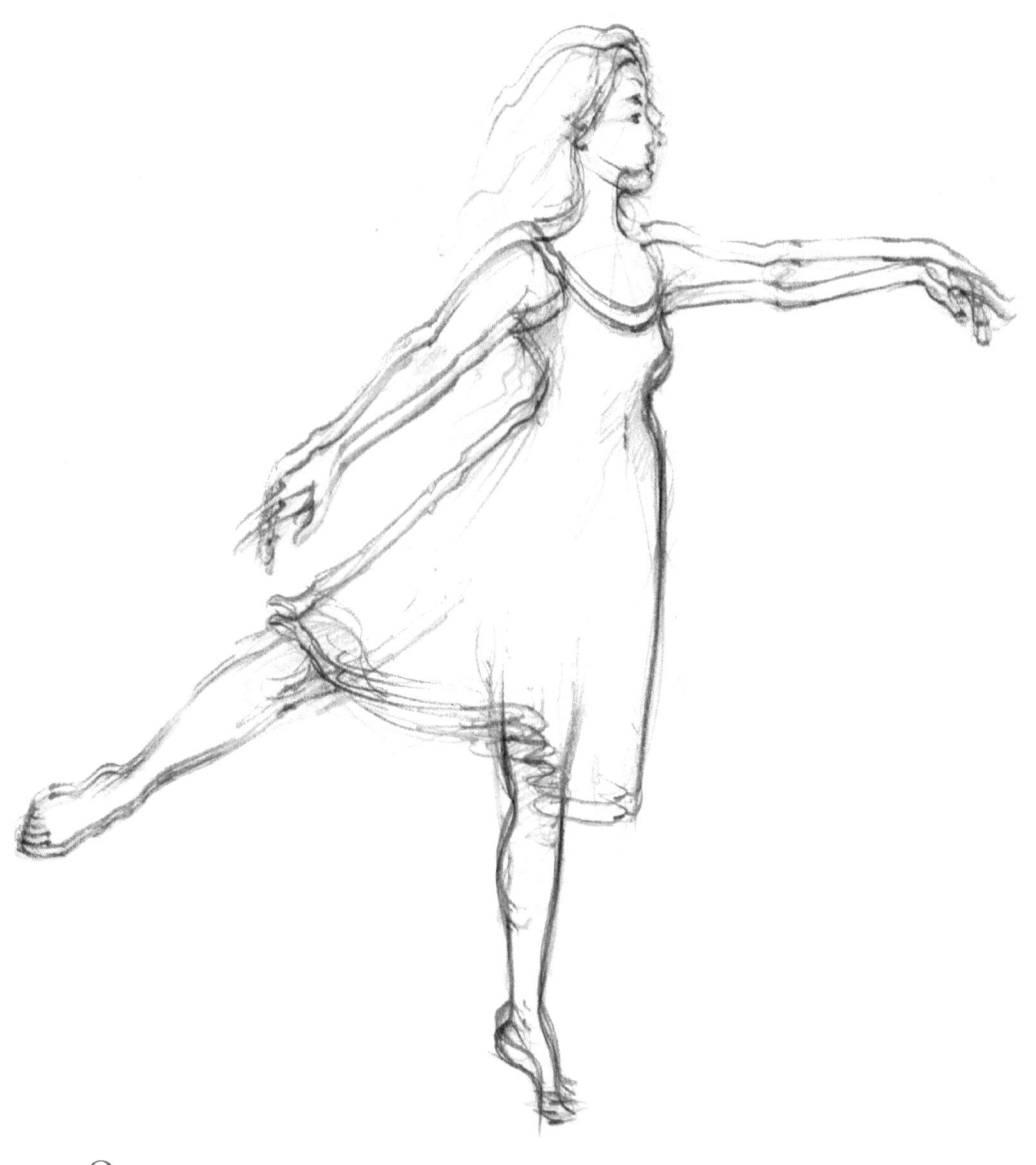

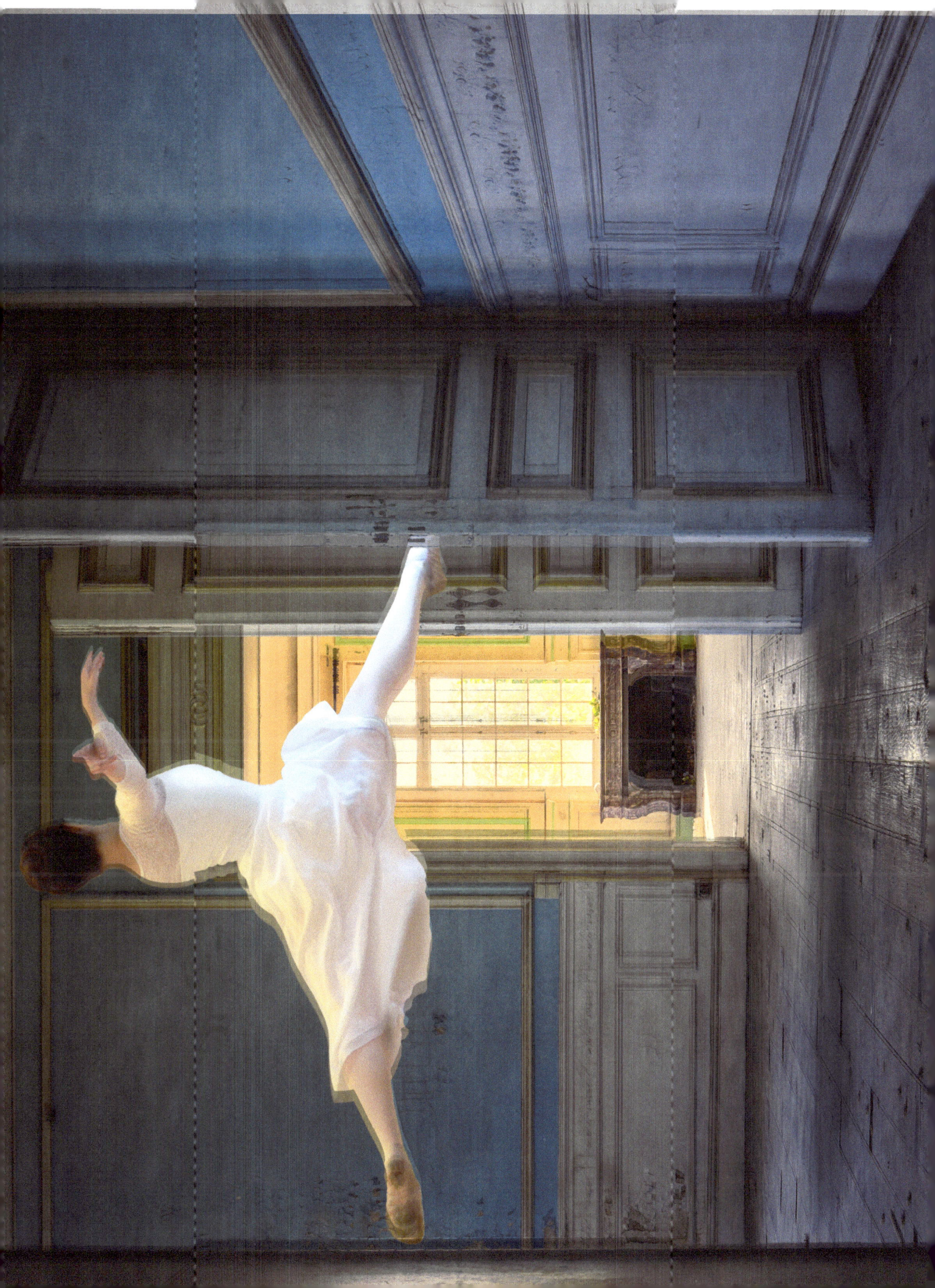

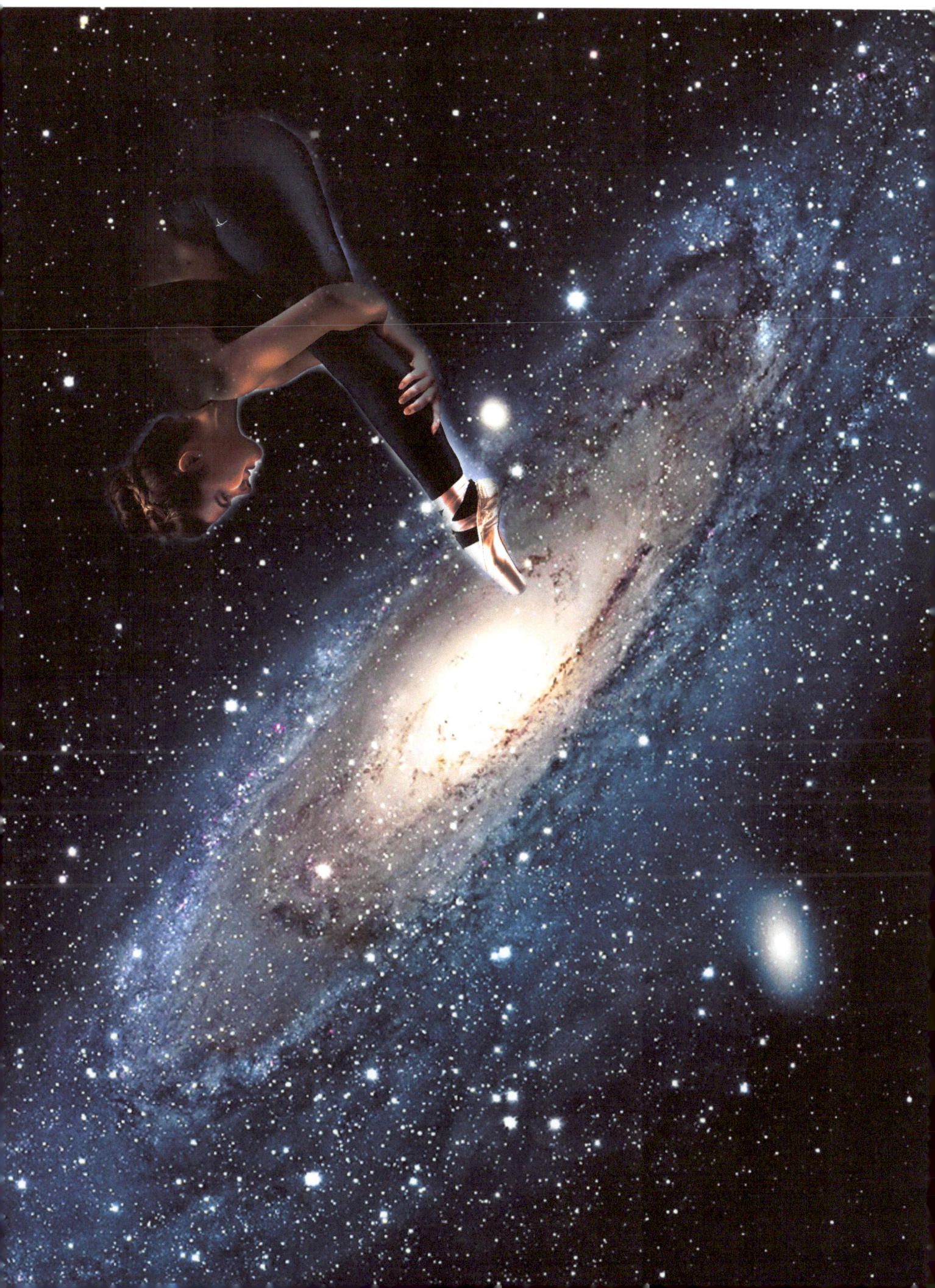

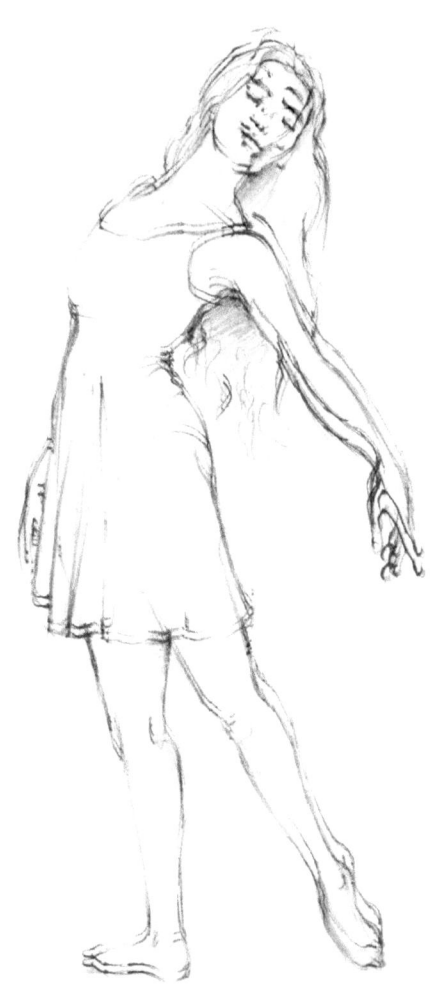

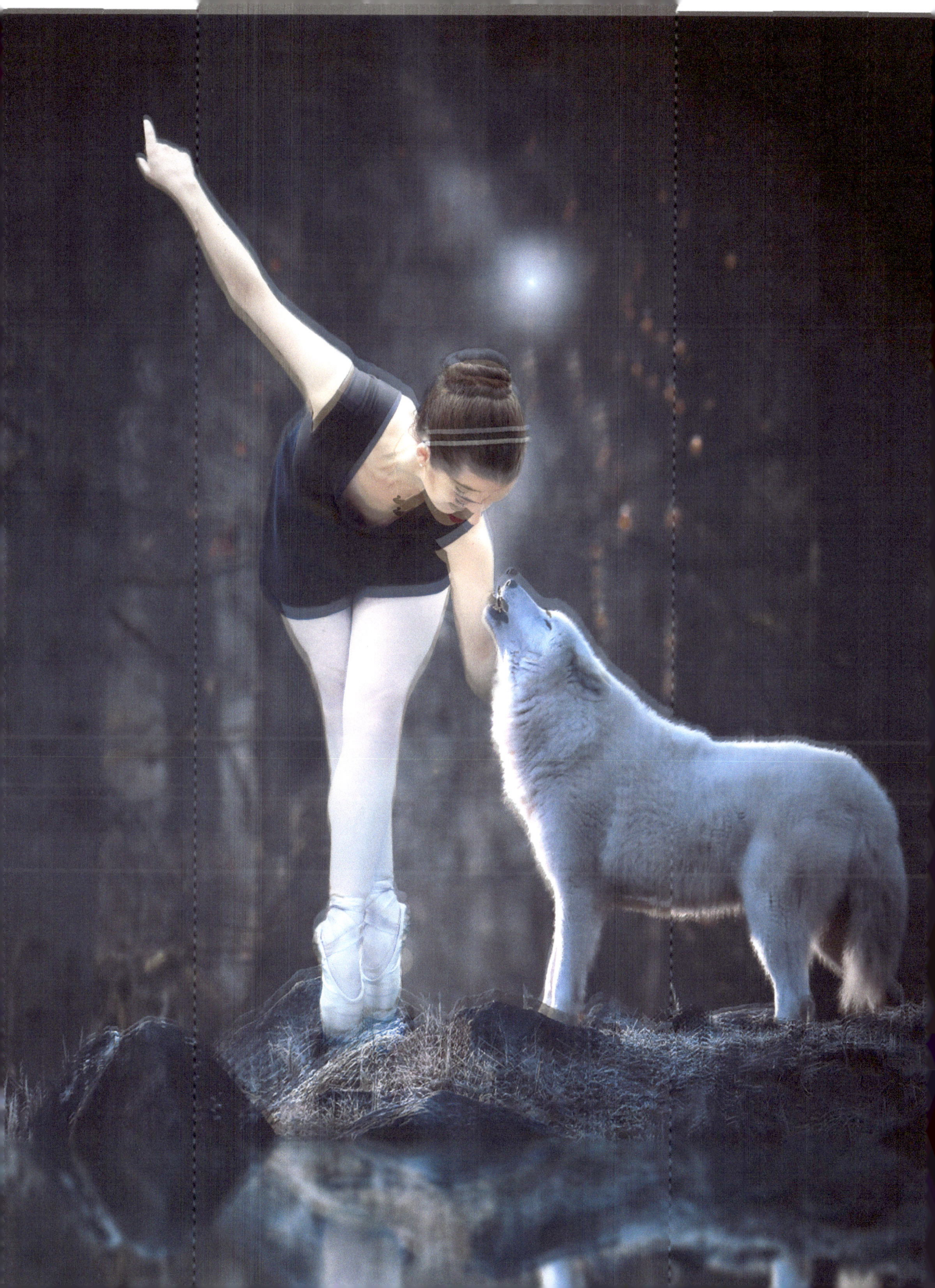

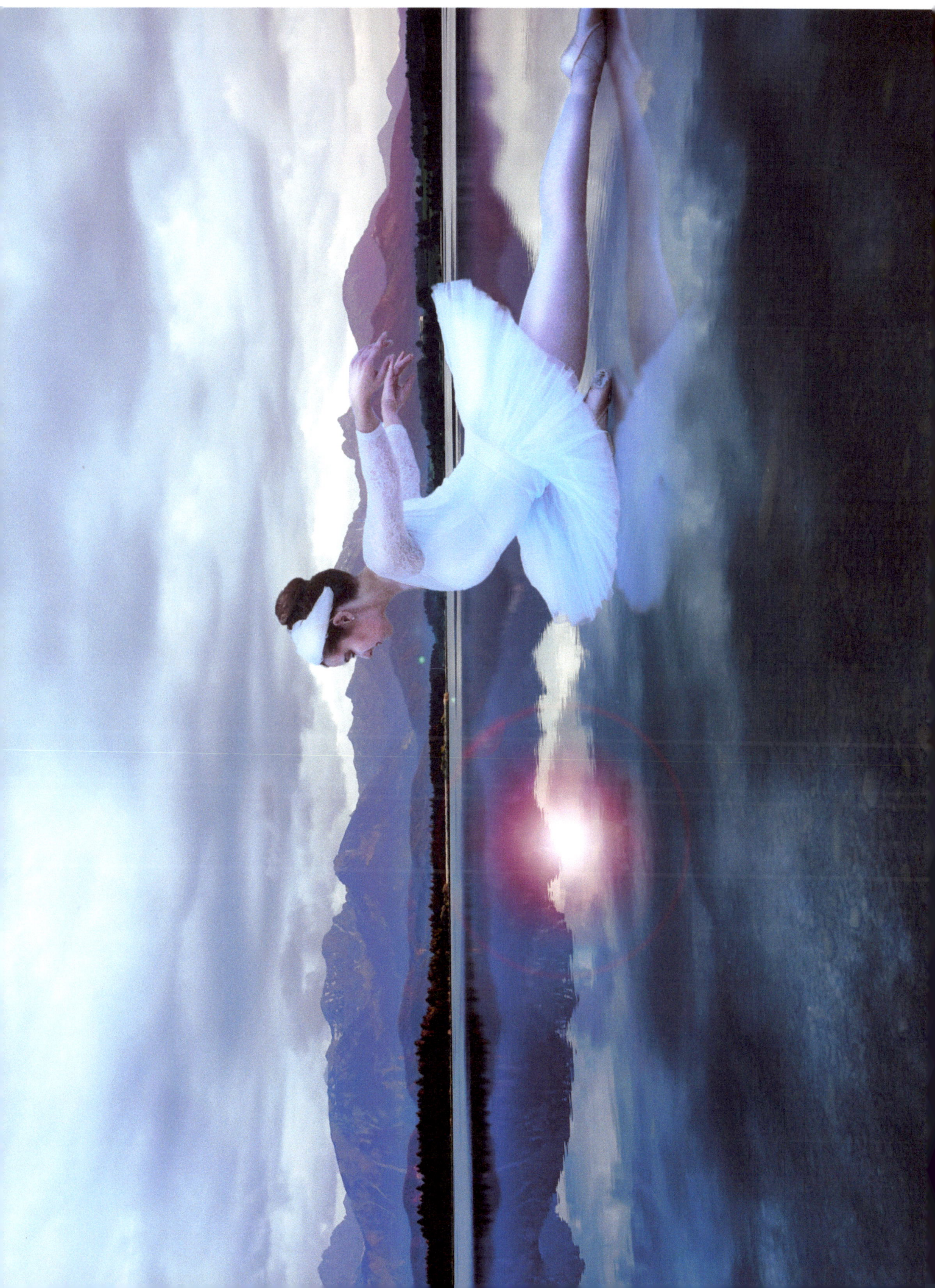

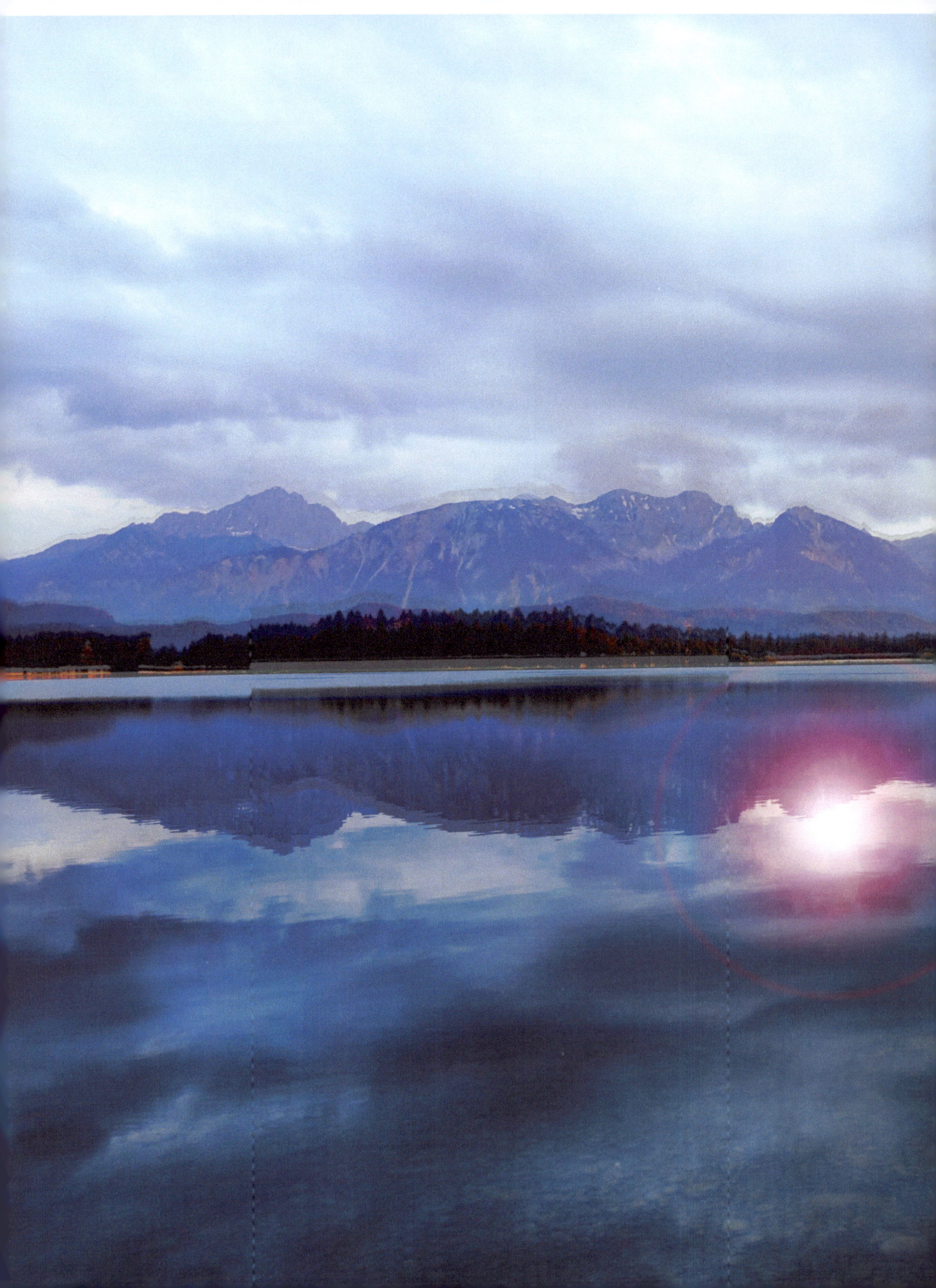

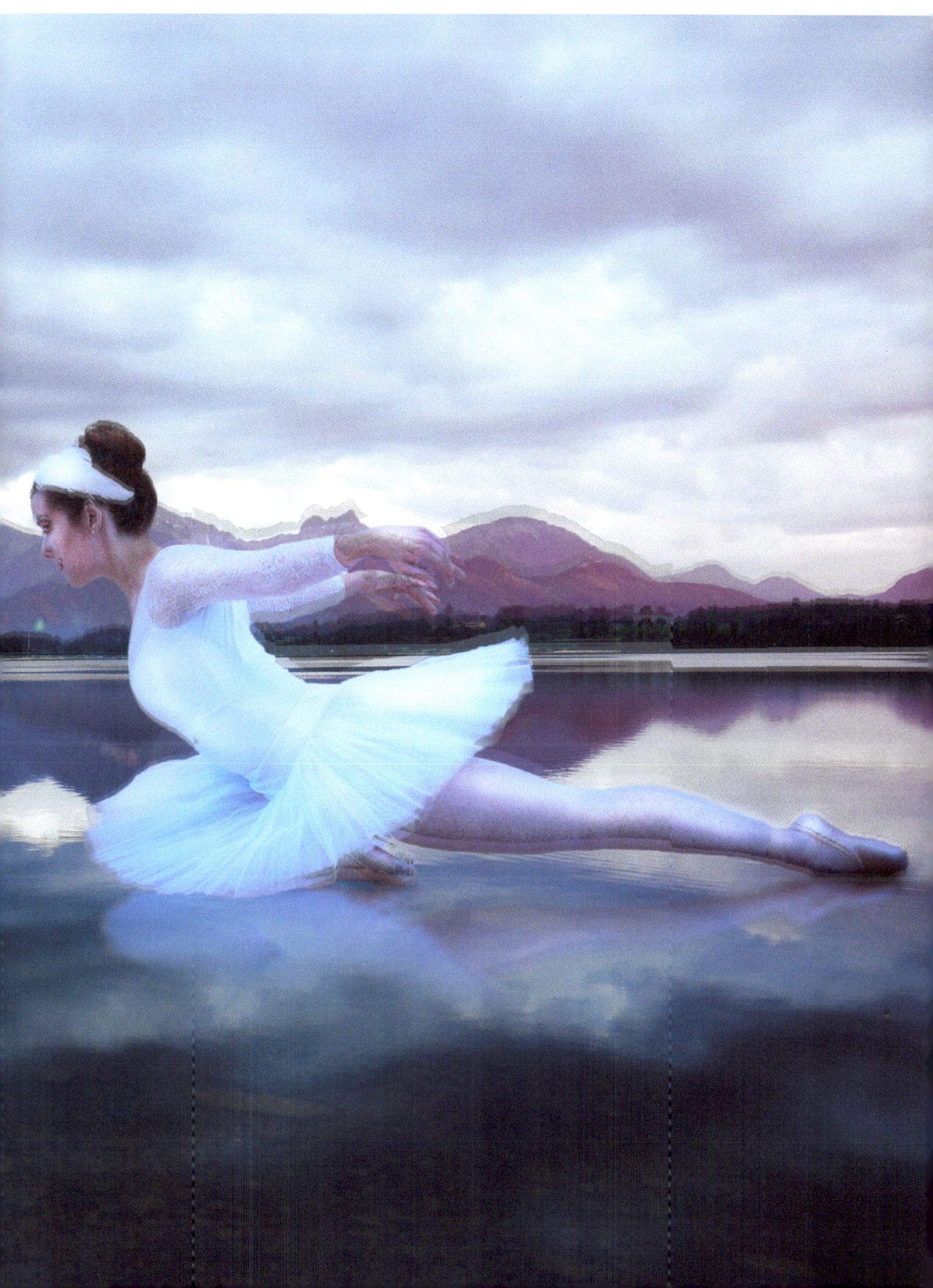

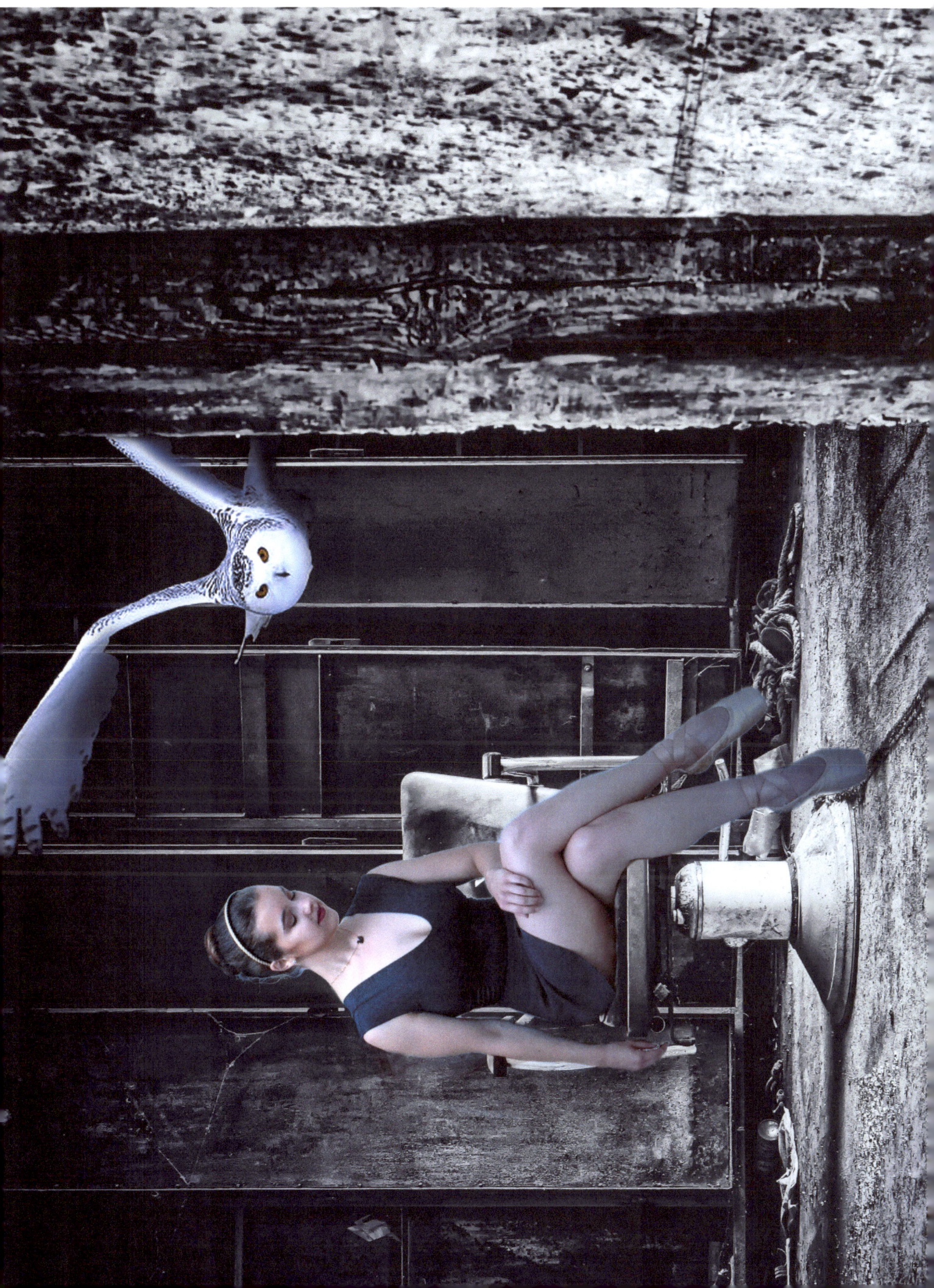

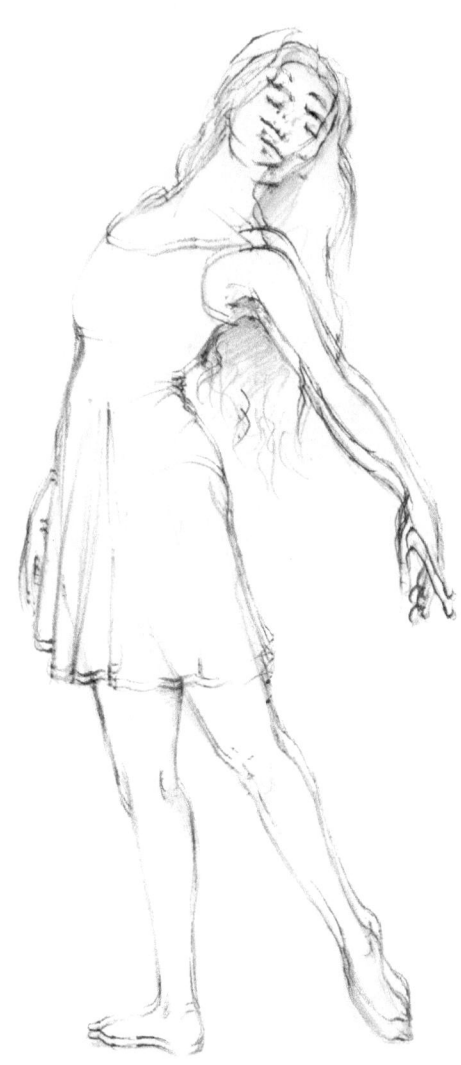

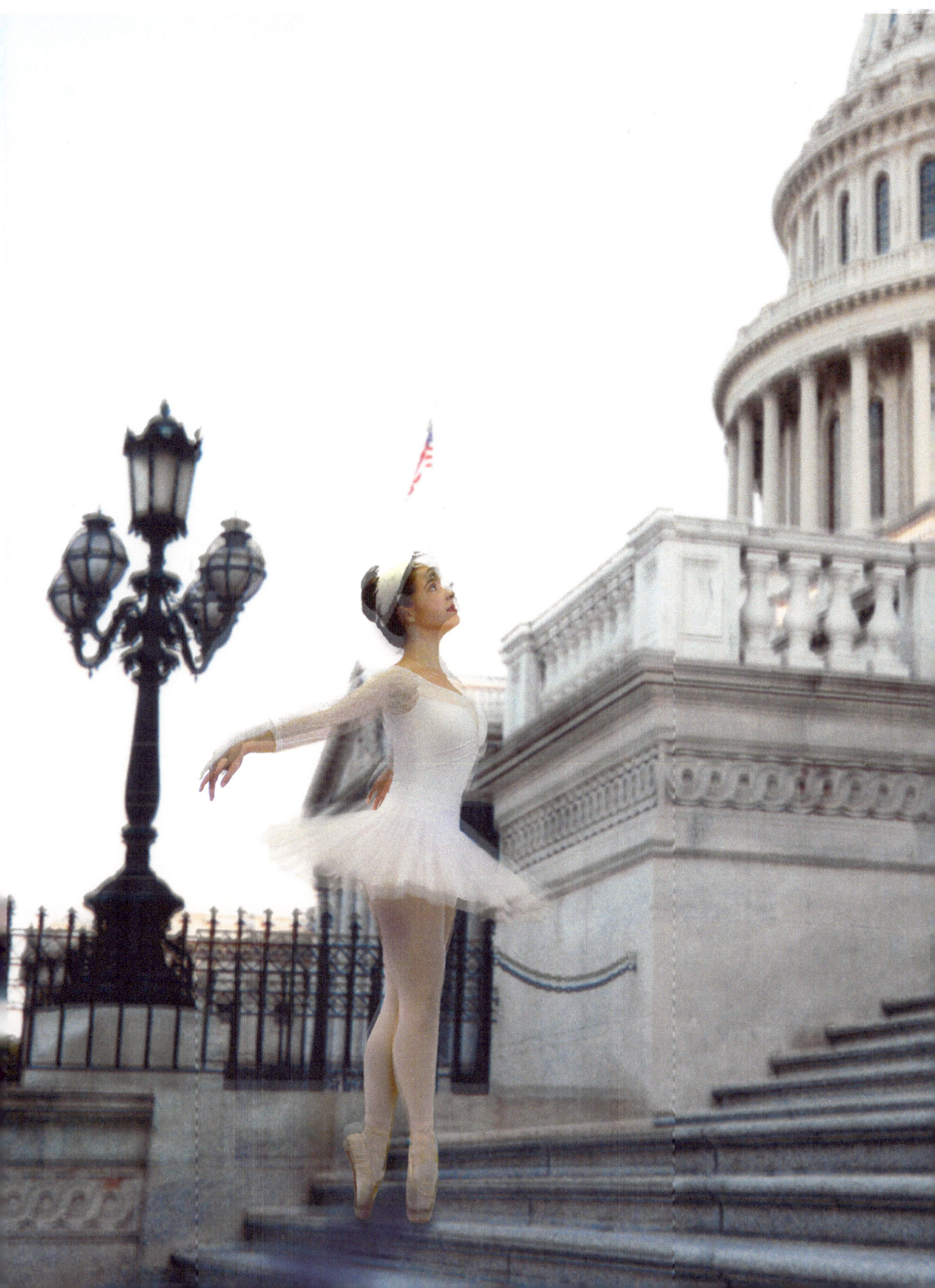

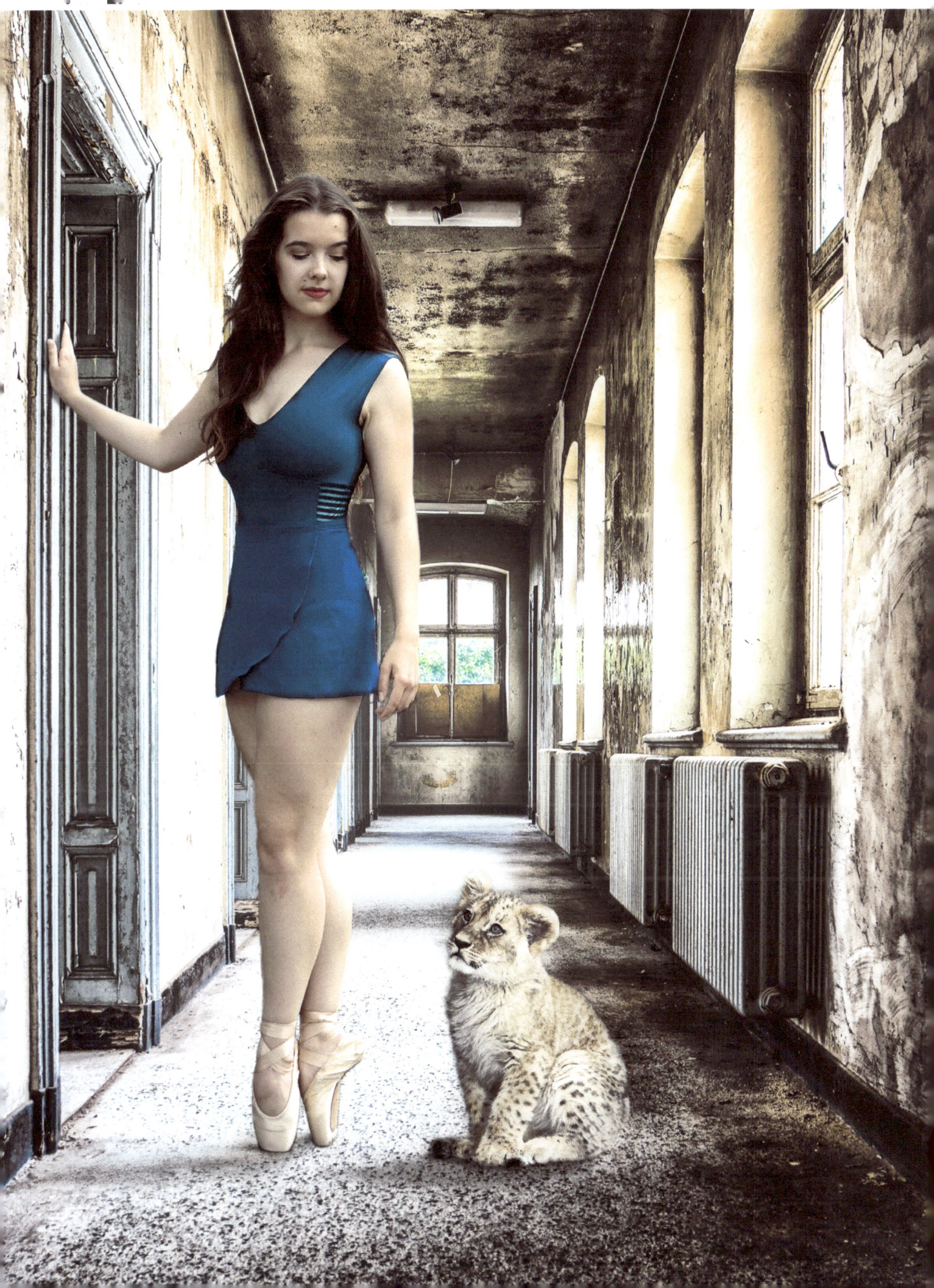

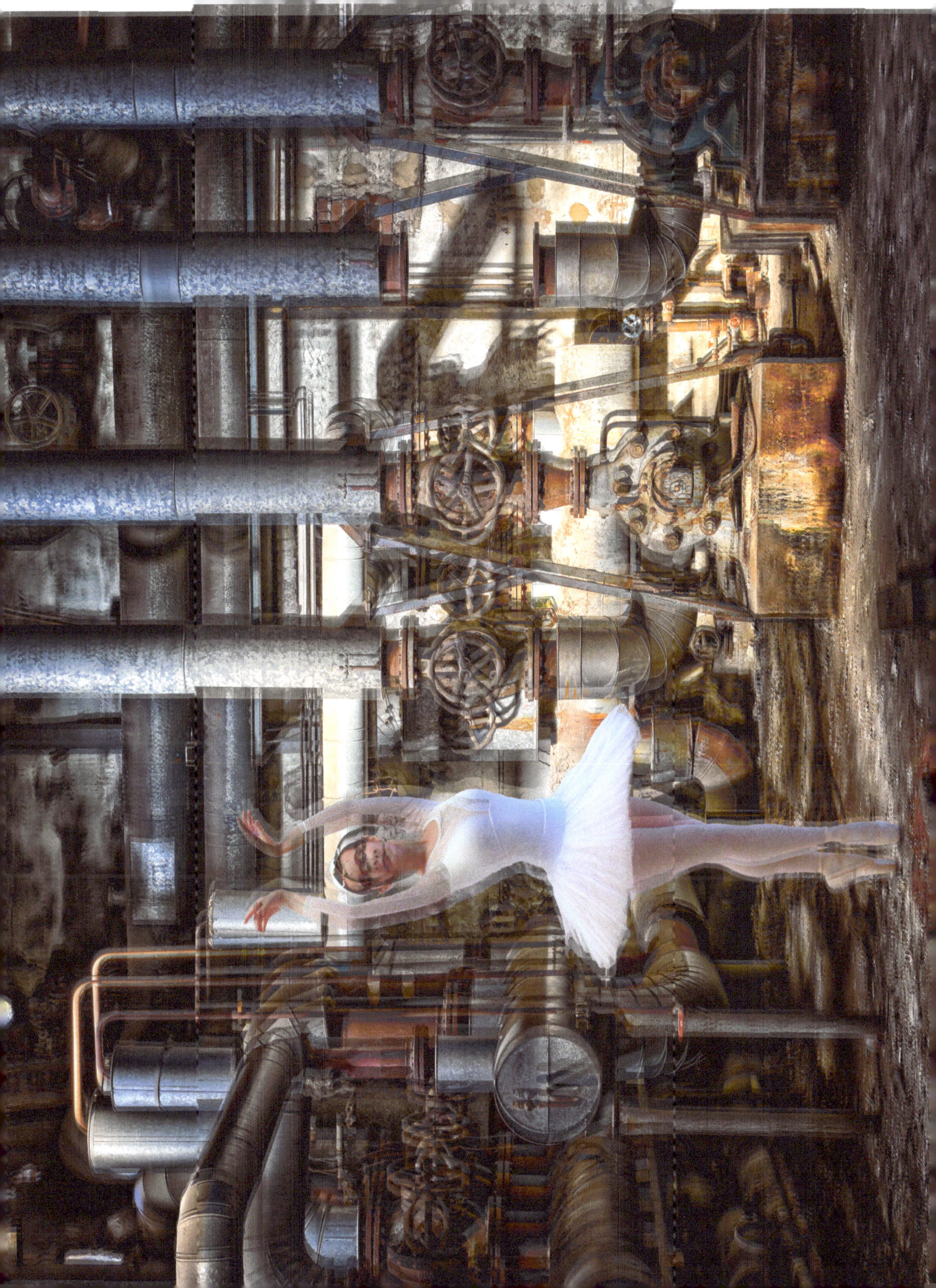

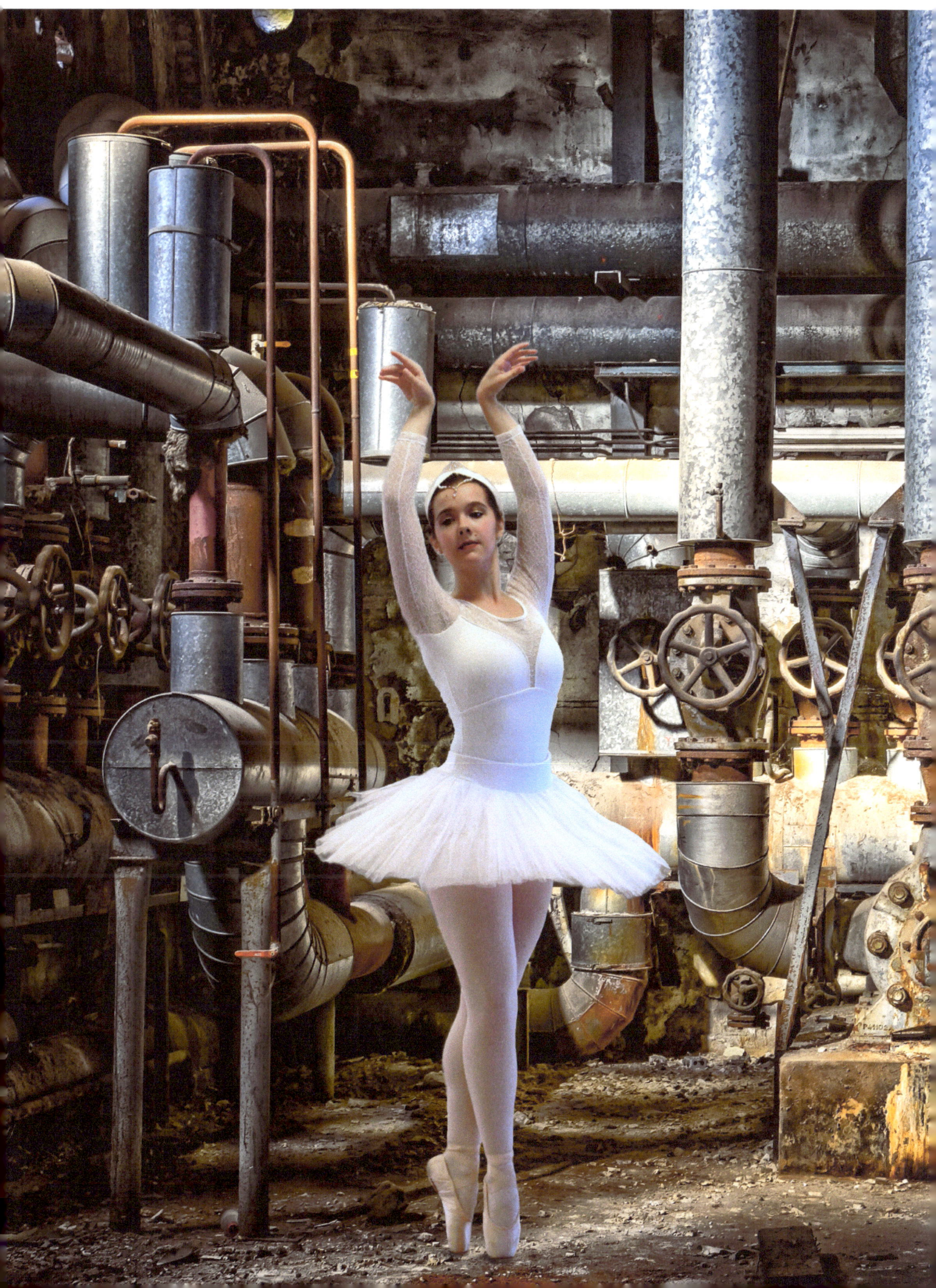

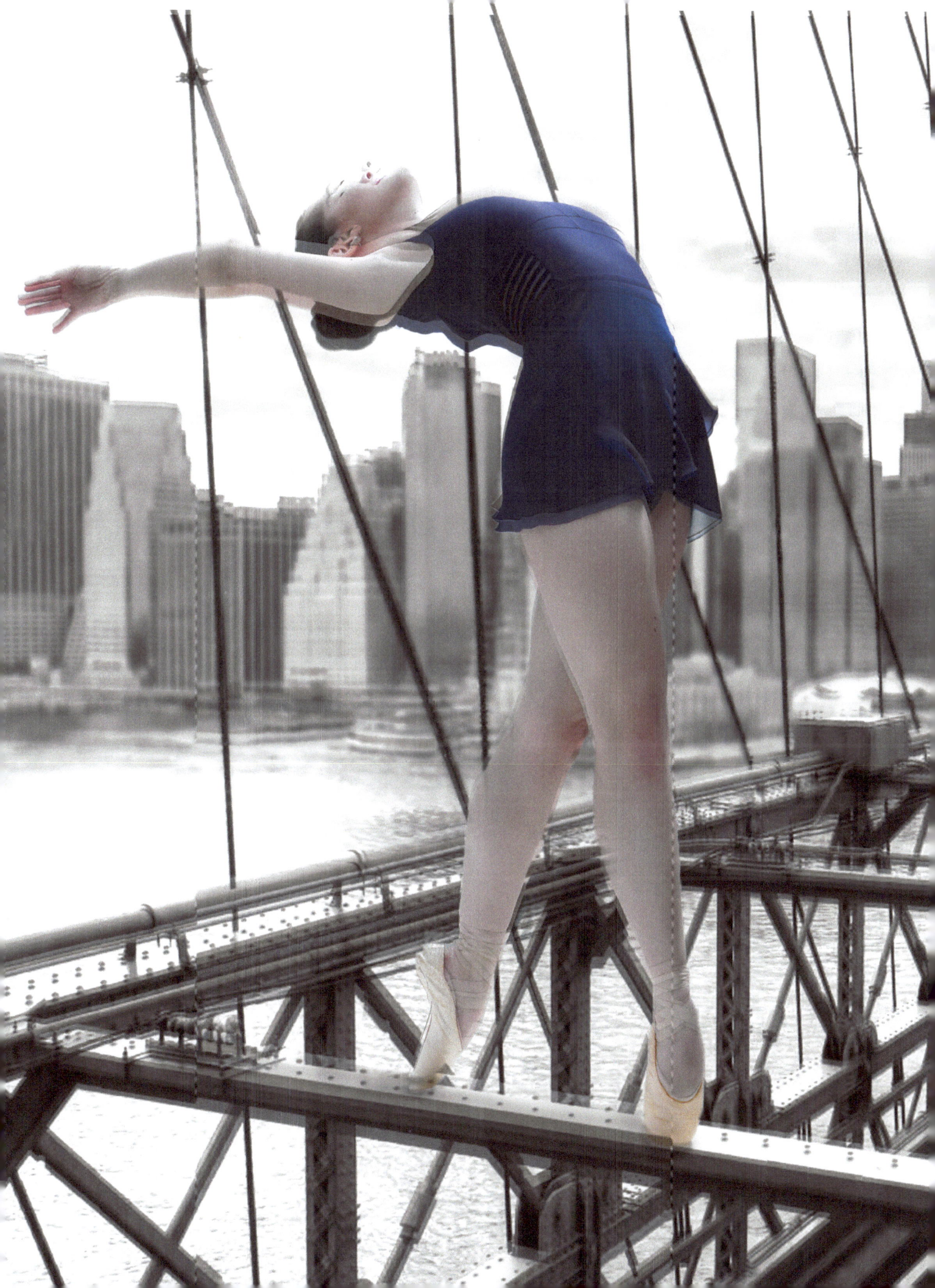

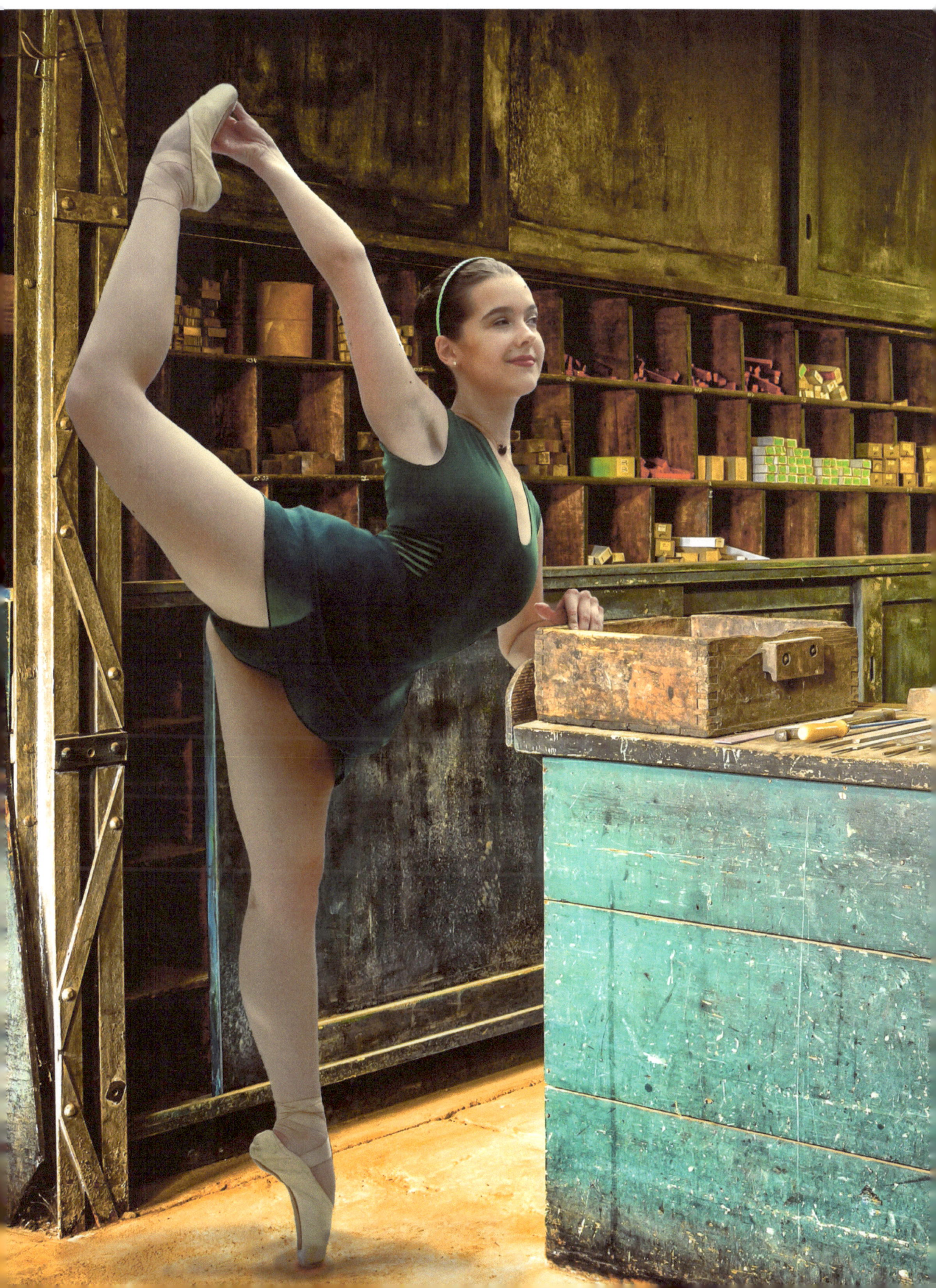

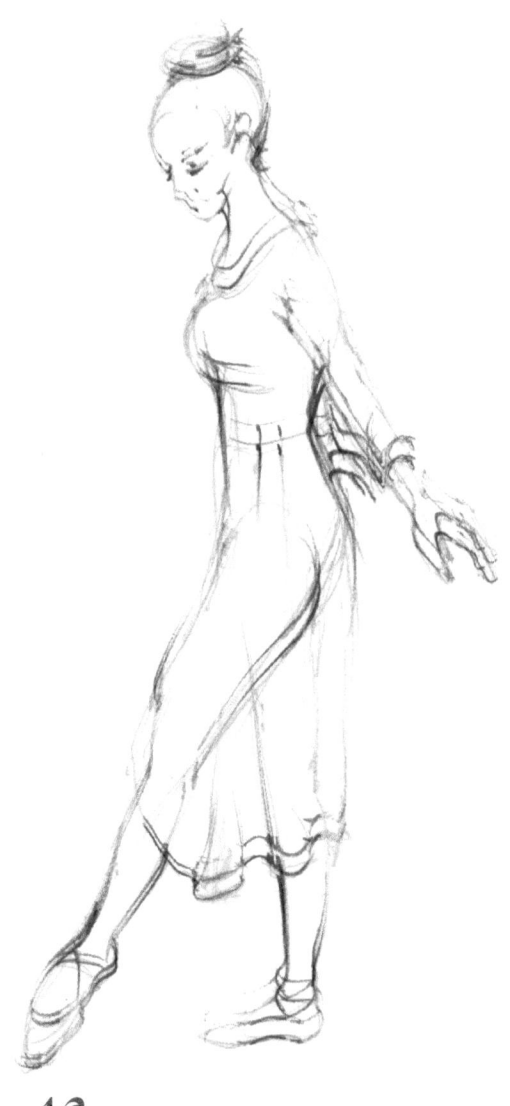

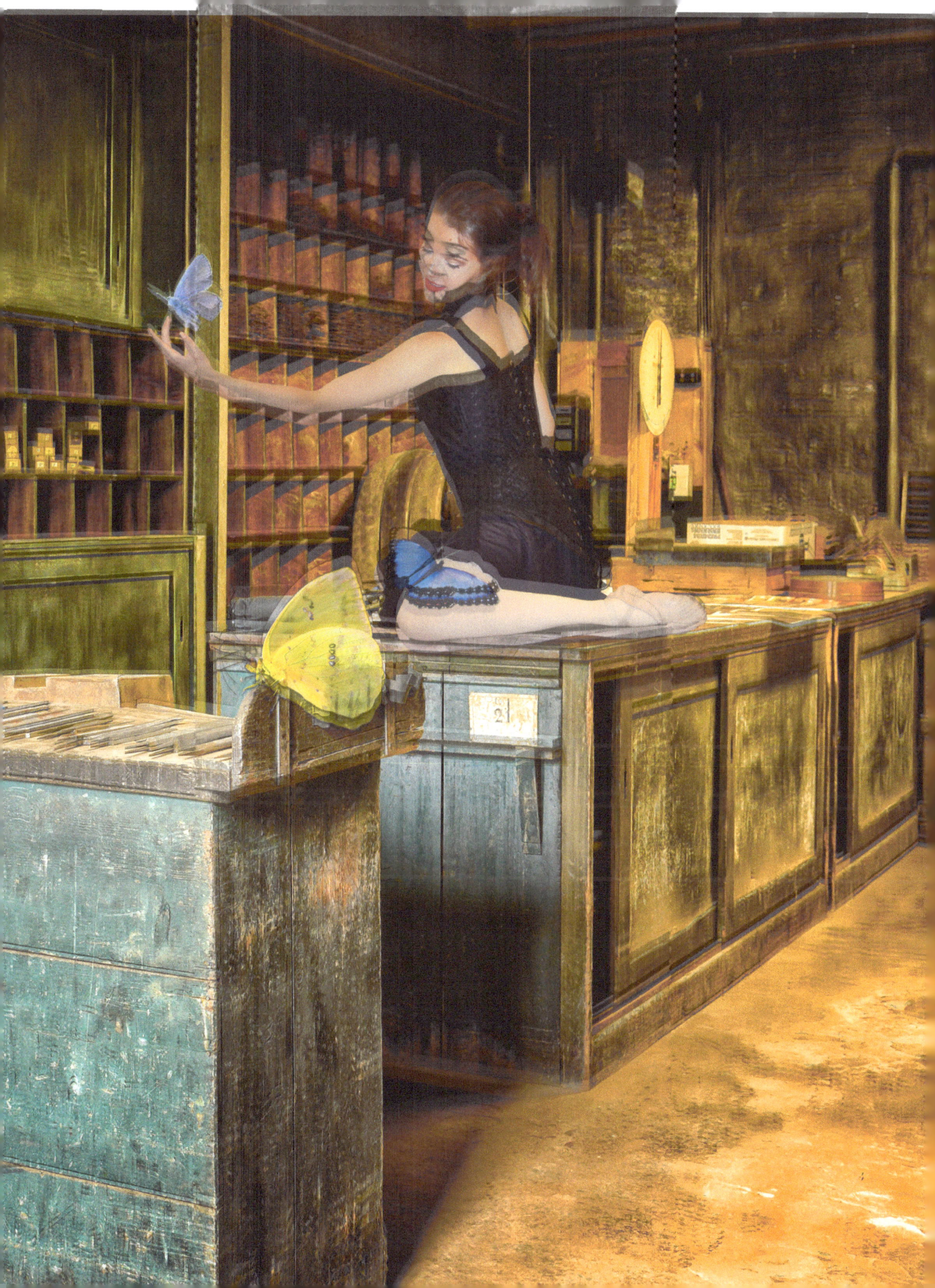

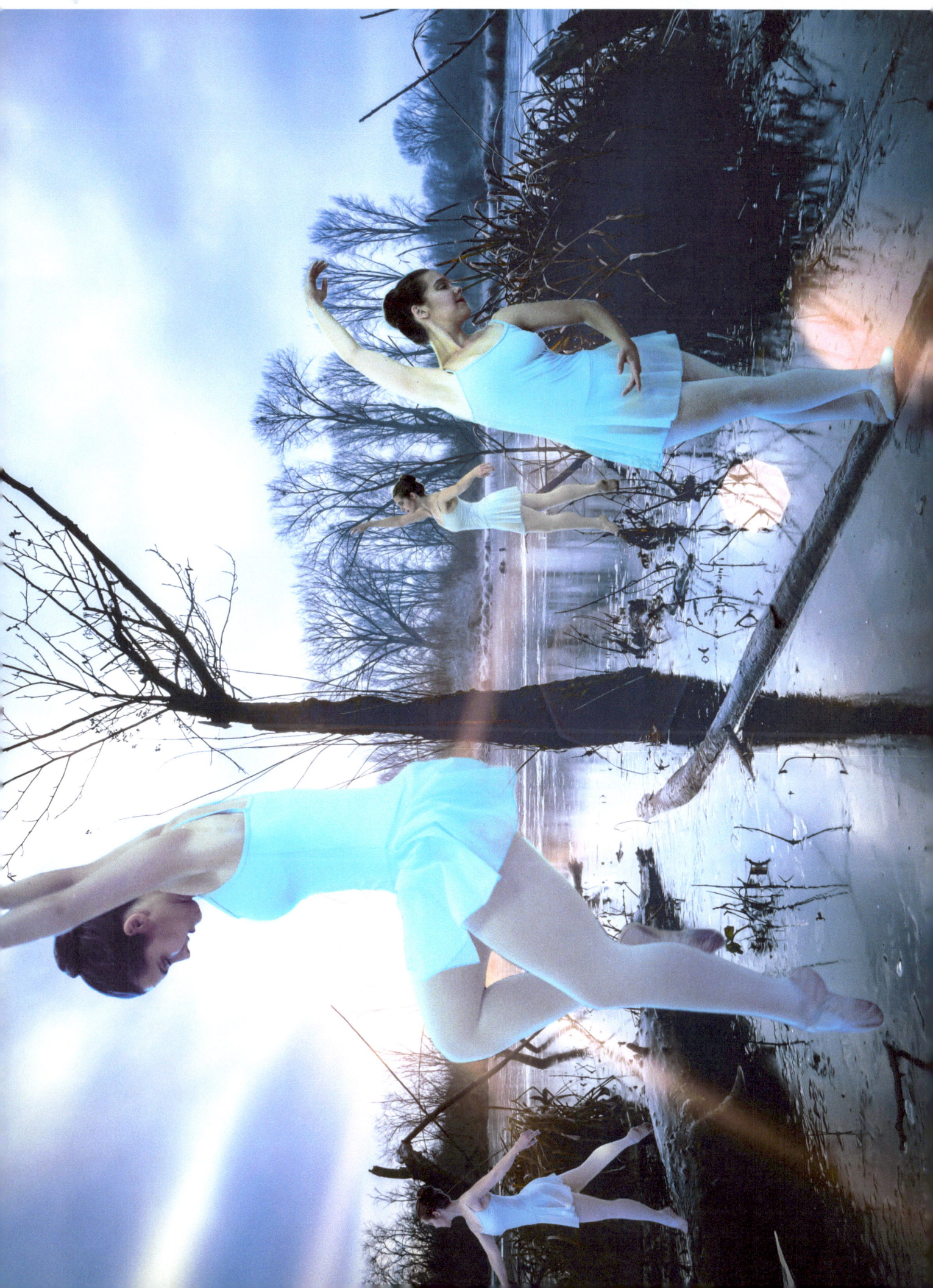

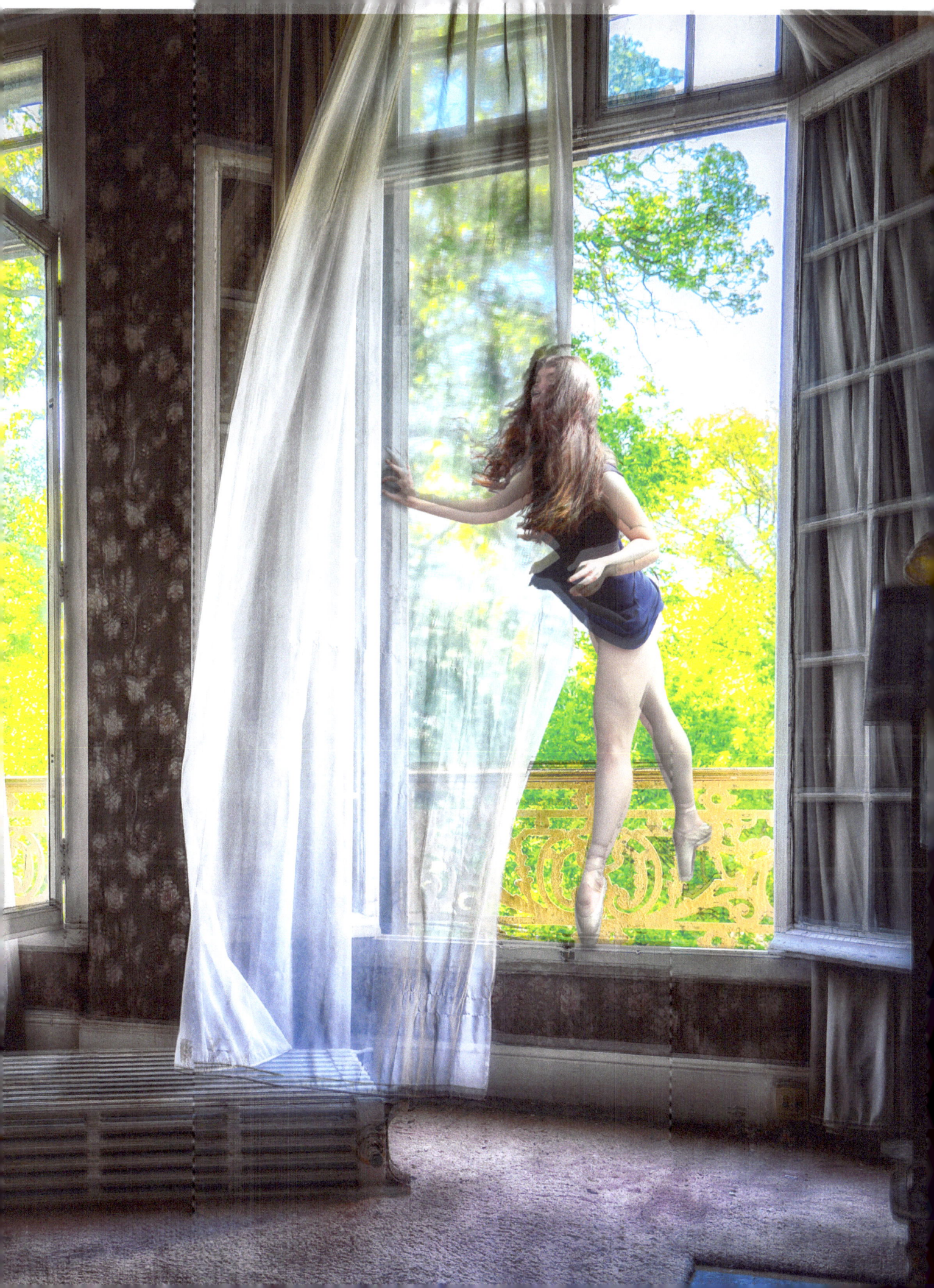

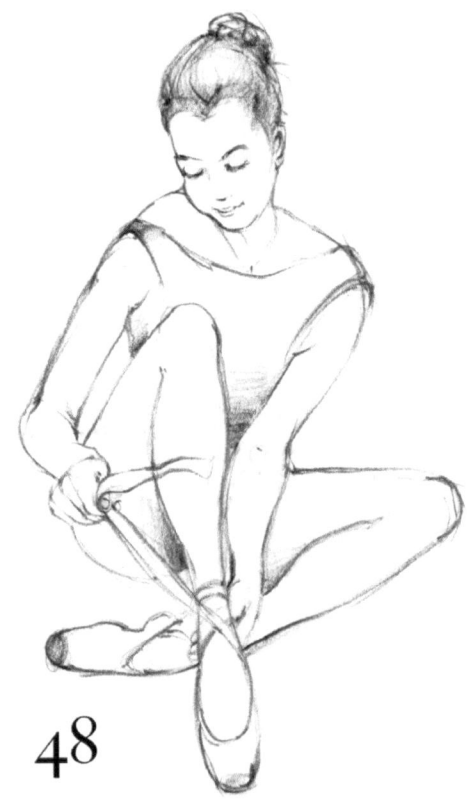

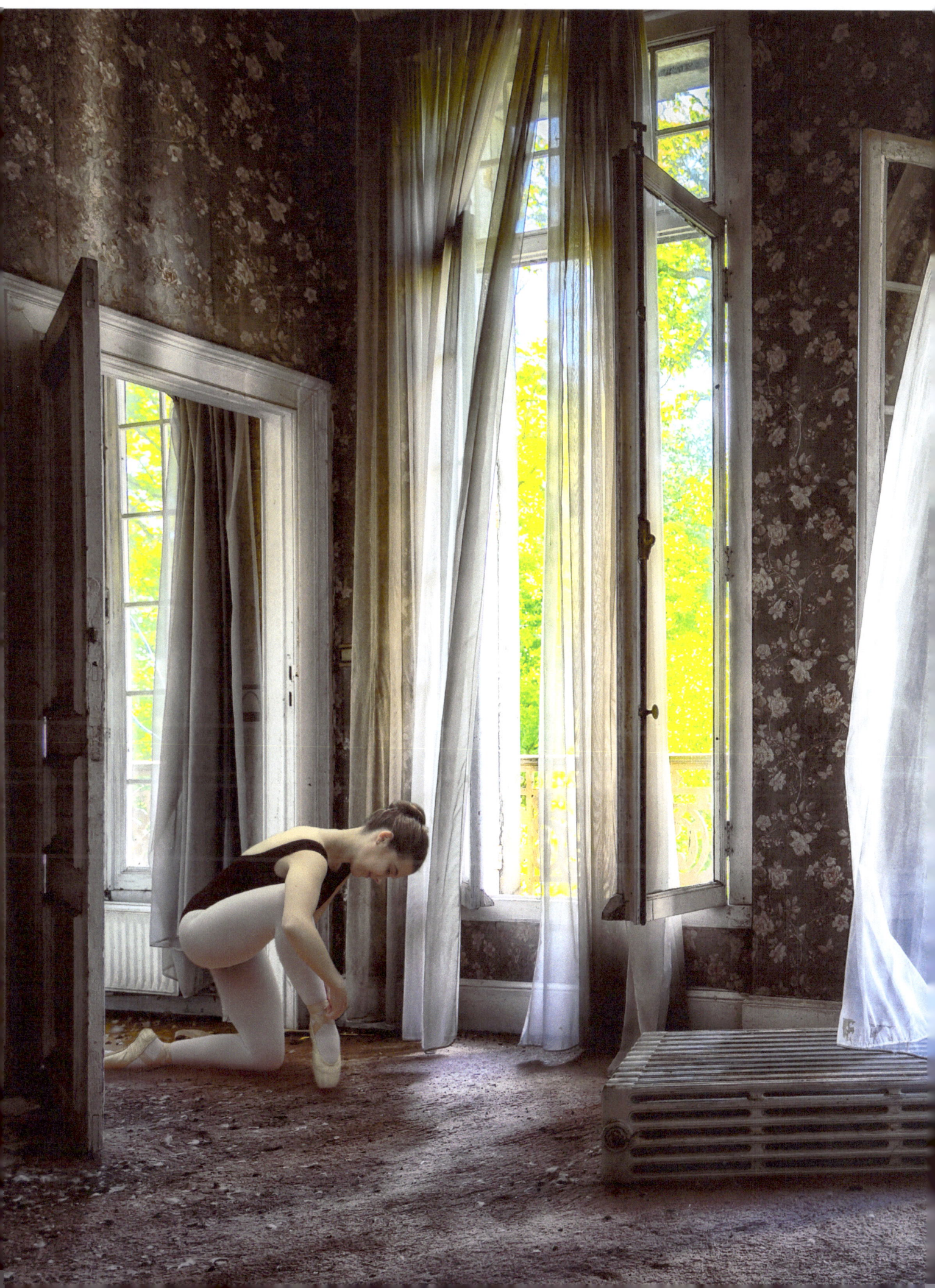

50

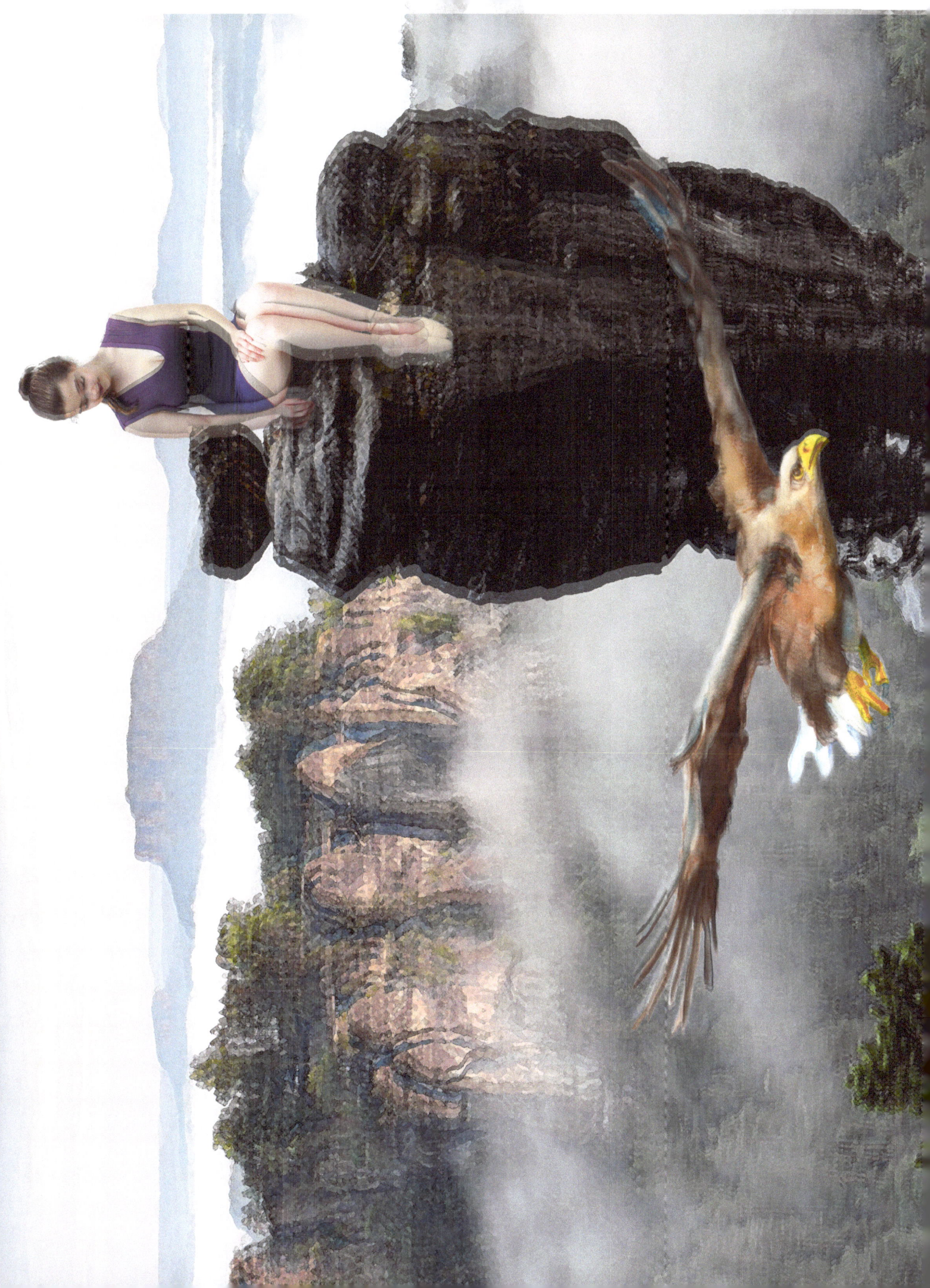

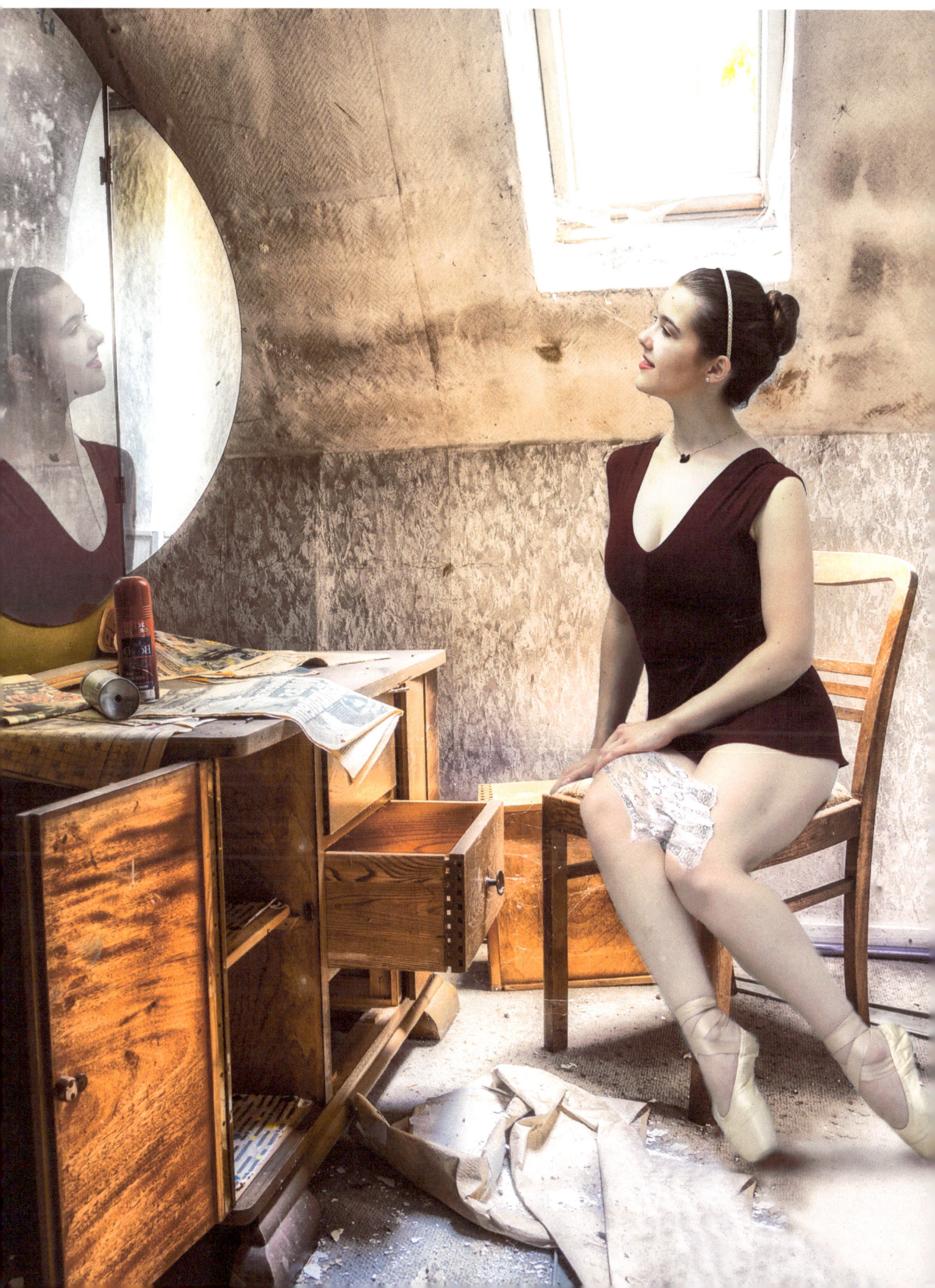

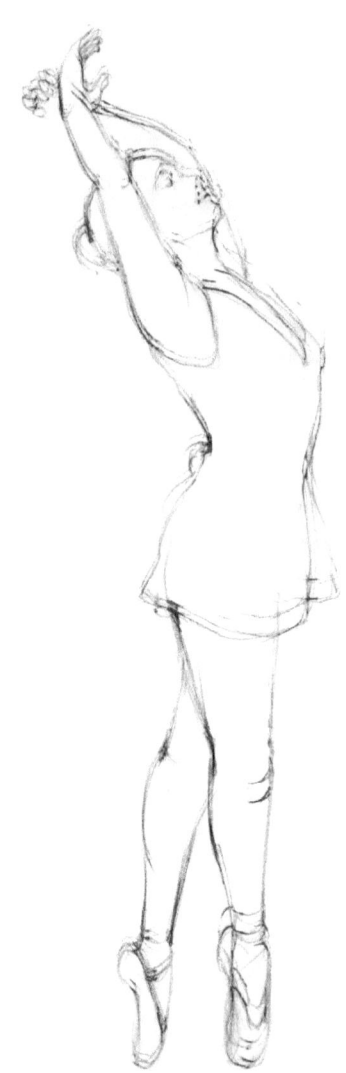

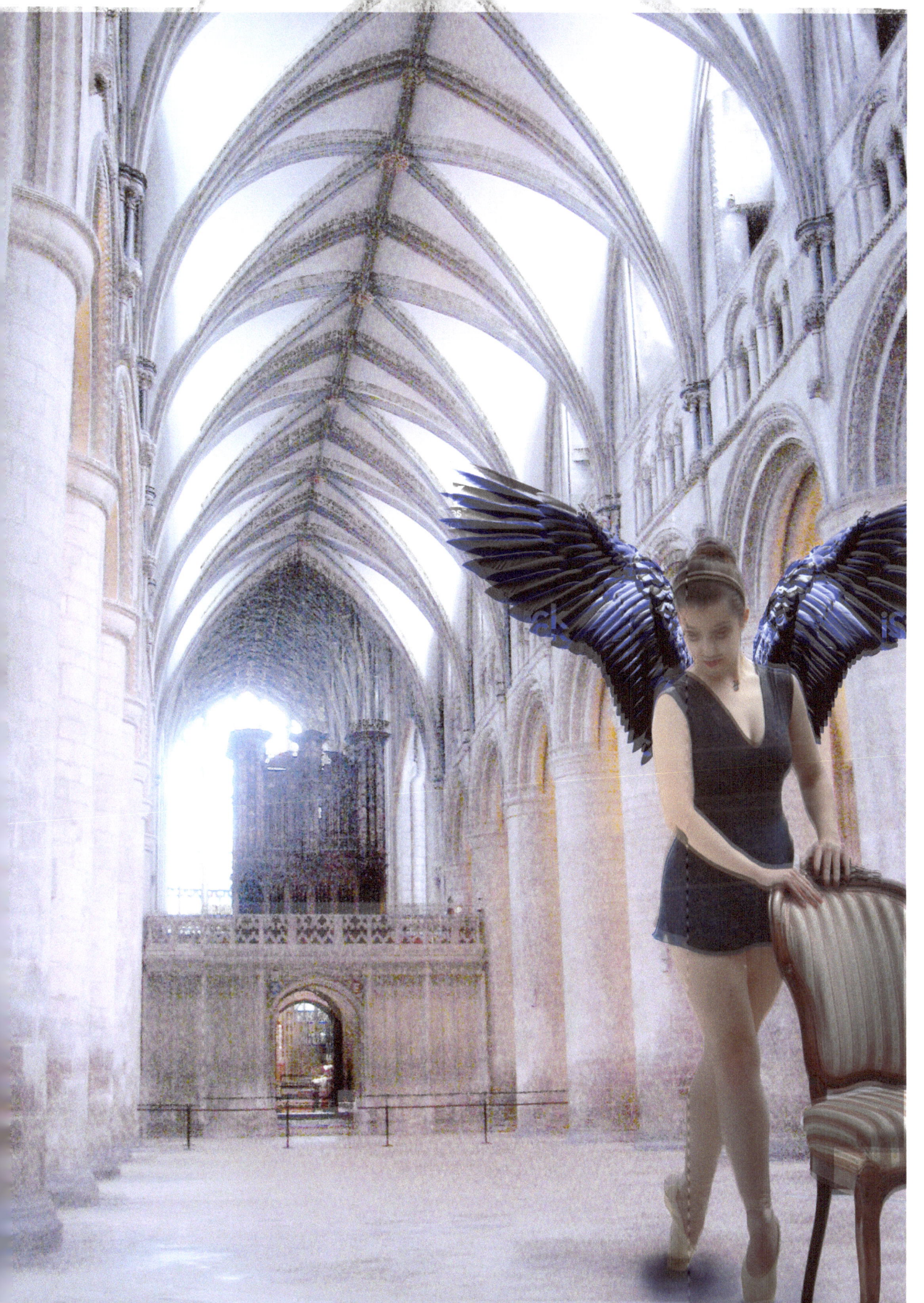

Making of

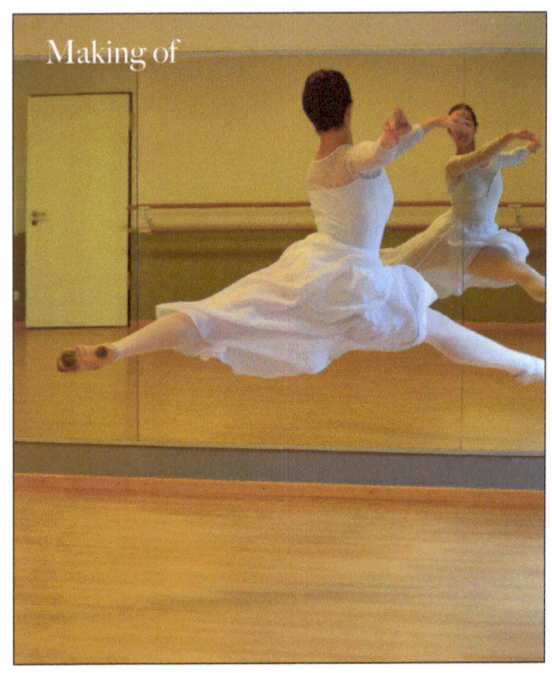
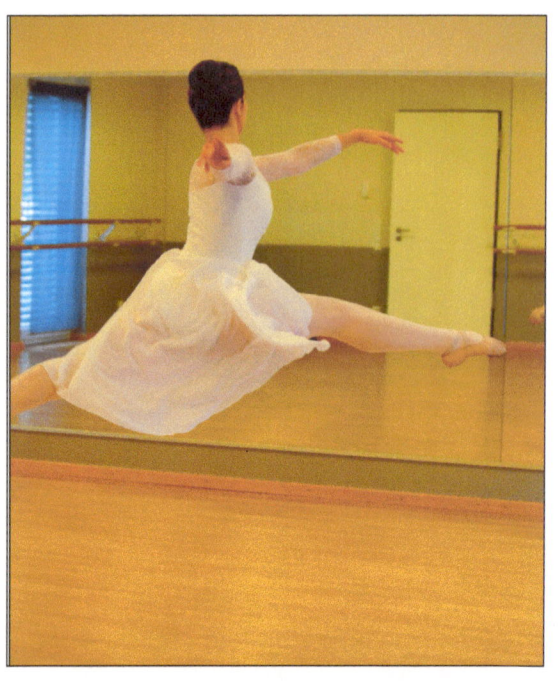
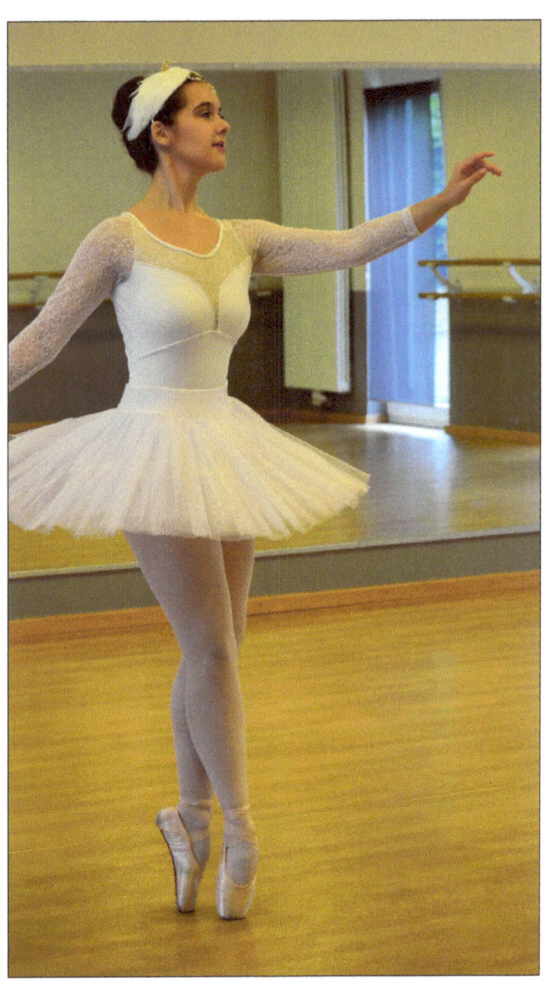
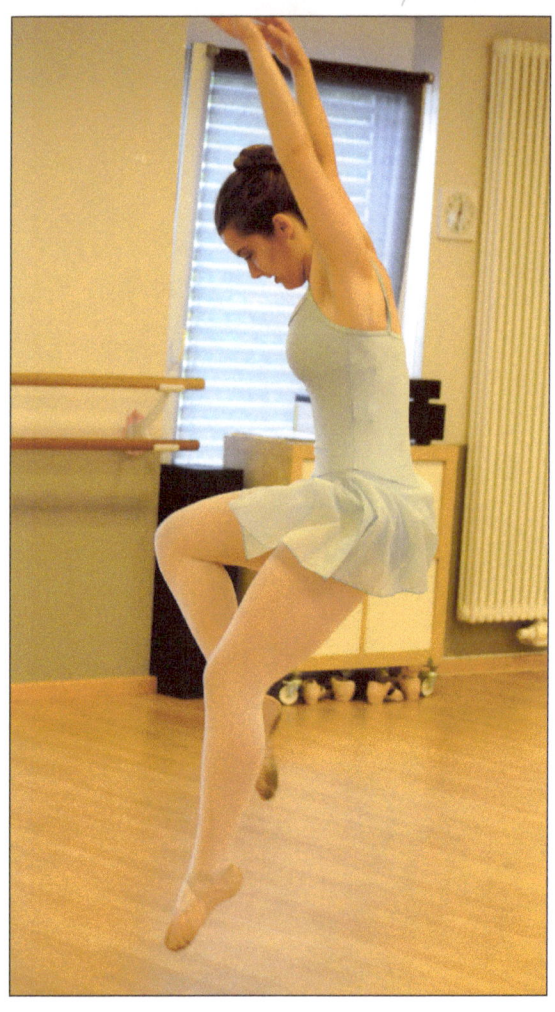

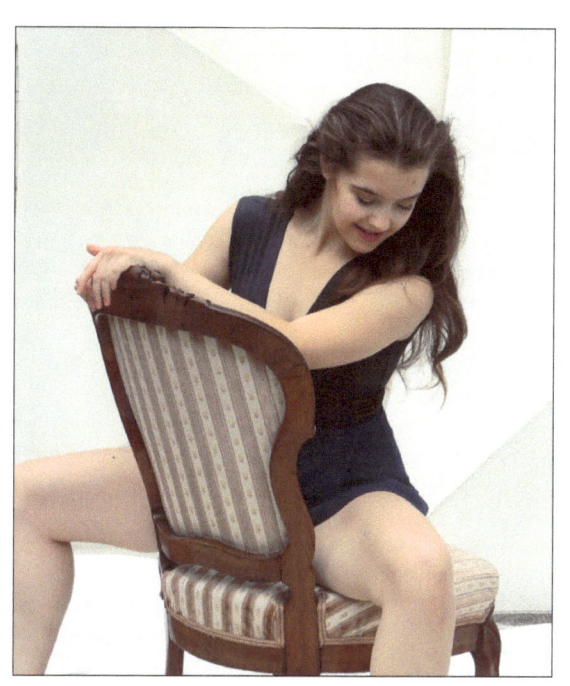
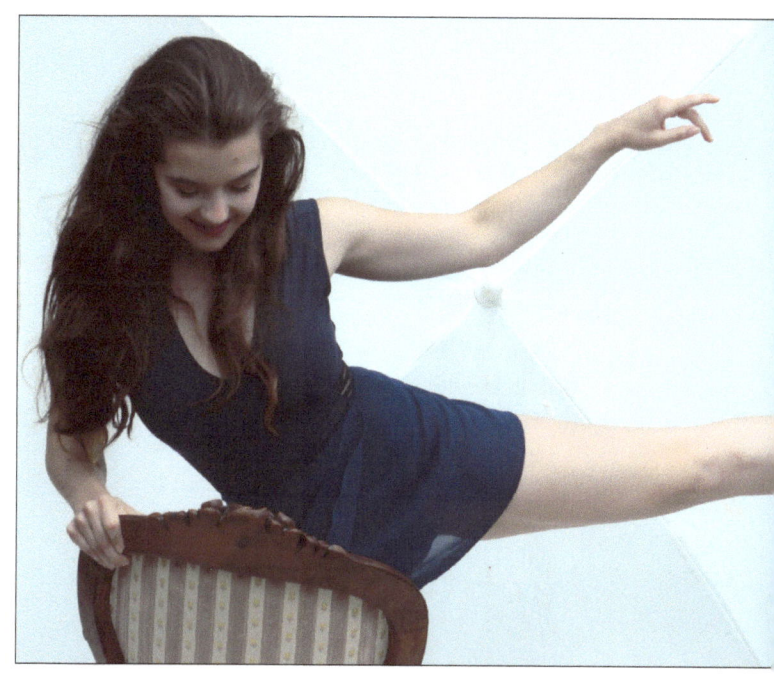
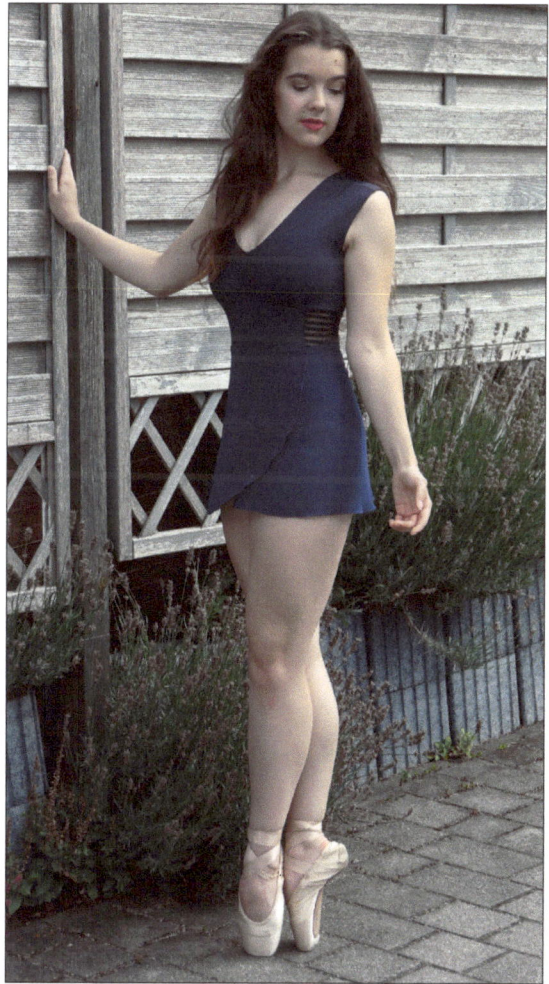
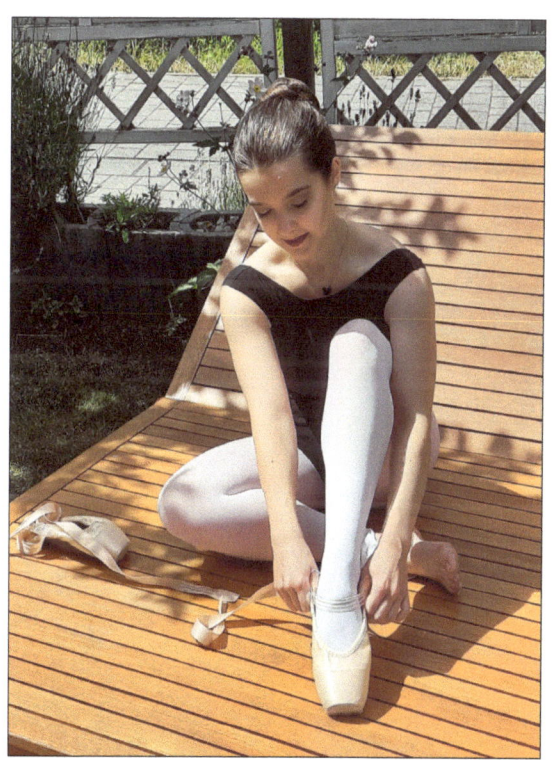

Bildnachweis

Herzlichen Dank an Peter Herrmann
für die Fotos der Hintergründe
auf den Seiten 6-9, 13, 14 und 17, 19, 29, 33,
35 und 37, 41 und 43, 45 und 47, 49 und 51, 55
auf Instagram: tiefstapler66

Montage S. 5:
Julius Kandler

Hintergrundfoto auf S. 31:
Uwe Fiebrich-Kandler

Illustration und Foto S. 53:
Cornelia Kandler

Image credits

Many thanks to Peter Herrmann
for the photos of the backgrounds
on pages 6-9, 13, 14 and 17, 19, 29, 33,
35 and 37, 41 and 43, 45 and 47, 49 and 51, 55
on Instagram: tiefstapler66

Montage p. 5:
Julius Kandler

Background photo on p. 31:
Uwe Fiebrich-Kandler

Illustration and photo p. 53:
Cornelia Kandler

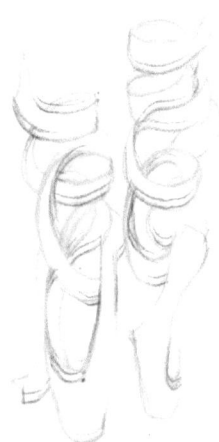

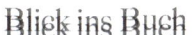

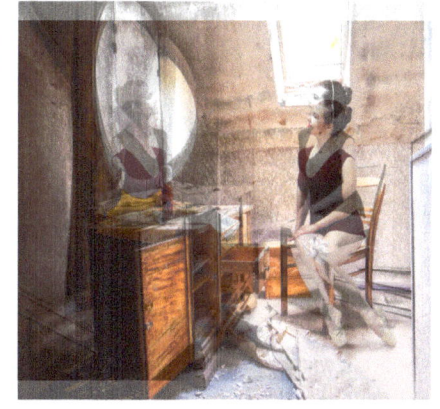
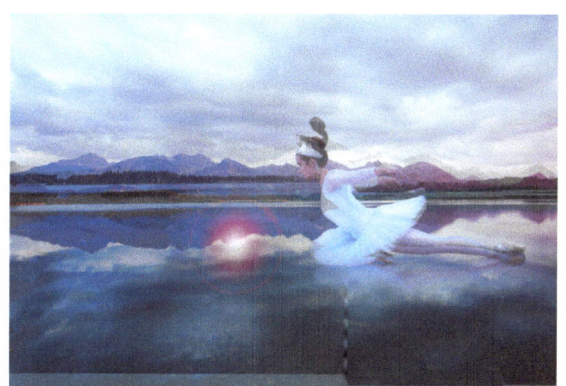
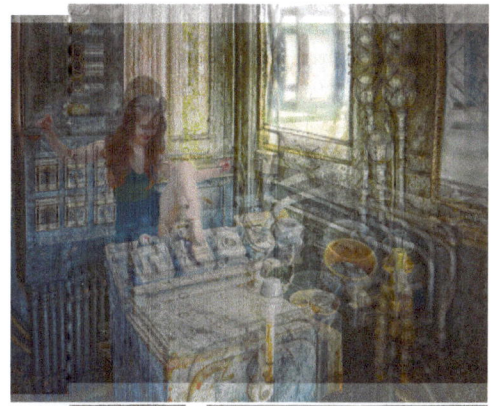
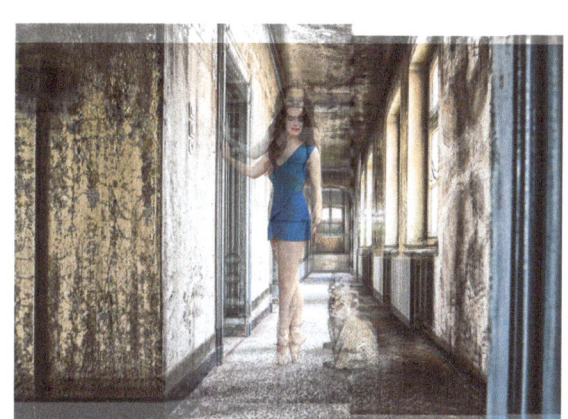
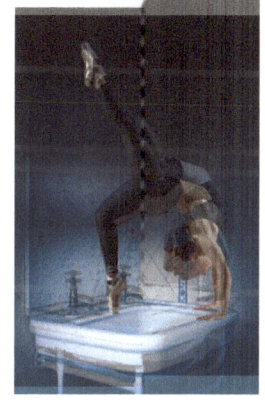
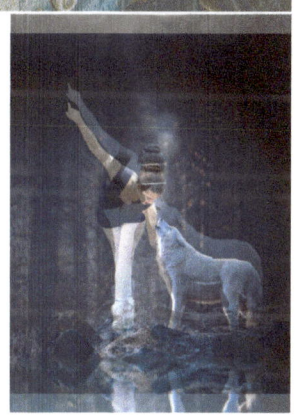
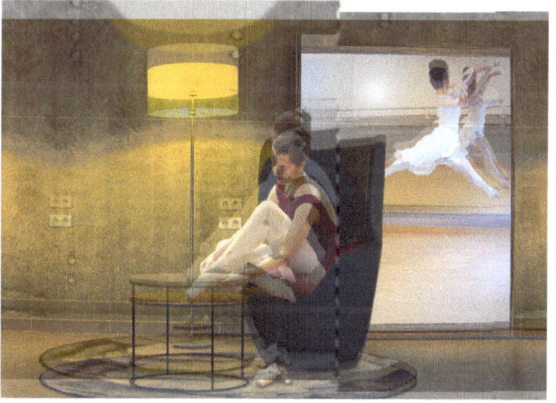
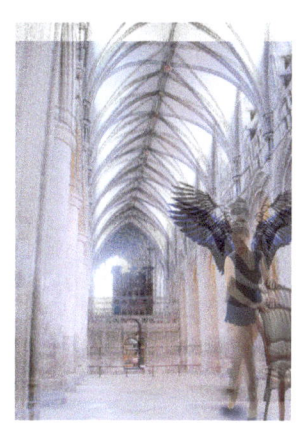
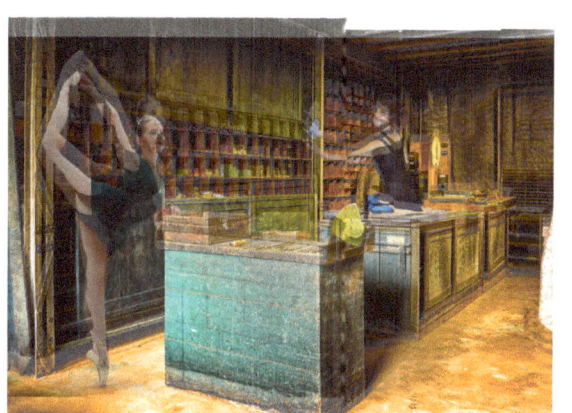